Asking them Questions

New Series

PART II

Also edited by Ronald Selby Wright

Asking Them Questions (1936)
Asking Them Questions, Second Series (1938)
Asking Why (1939)
Soldiers Also Asked (1943)
Asking Them Questions, Third Series (1950)
Asking Them Questions: A Selection from the
    First Three Series (1953)
Fathers of the Kirk (1960)
A Manual of Church Doctrine according to the
    Church of Scotland (with T. F. Torrance, 1960)
Asking Them Questions: New Series; Part I (1972)

By Ronald Selby Wright

Take Up God's Armour (1967)

Asking them Questions

New Series

PART II

'They found Him . . . sitting in the
midst of the doctors, both hearing
them, and asking them questions.'
LUKE 2:46

EDITED BY

Ronald Selby Wright

LONDON
OXFORD UNIVERSITY PRESS
New York   Toronto
1972

Oxford University Press, Ely House, London W.1

GLASGOW NEW YORK TORONTO MELBOURNE WELLINGTON
CAPE TOWN IBADAN NAIROBI DAR ES SALAAM LUSAKA ADDIS ABABA
DELHI BOMBAY CALCUTTA MADRAS KARACHI LAHORE DACCA
KUALA LUMPUR SINGAPORE HONG KONG TOKYO

ISBN 0 19 213424 8

© Oxford University Press, 1972

Set I.B.M. by George Over Ltd, London and Rugby
Printed in Great Britain by
Fletcher & Son Ltd. Harford Works Norwich

Dedicated to
JOAN E. WHITE
and
her colleagues at the
Oxford University Press

Acknowledgement

Thanks are due to Mr. John Murray and the author for permission to include the lines by Sir John Betjeman in the contribution by the Rev. Harry Williams.

Preface

This is the second Part of a New Series of which Part I has already been published. As stated in the Preface to Part I, the original series of *Asking Them Questions* owed its origin, as some readers may remember, to questions asked me by the then members of my Boys' Club, most of whom had in those days no Church connection, came from poor homes, and few, if any, I thought had any kind of real interest in religion. When, as I got to know them better, we began quite naturally to discuss the meaning and purpose of life as we camped together or sat around the Club fire, I found that the interest was very much there and that the kind of questions they asked were of a nature that greatly surprised me and required much more serious and considered answers than I, a young raw student, felt competent to give. And so, as much for my own help as for theirs, I sent some of the questions to good and scholarly men and asked if they could help, beginning with two of my own most admired teachers, Professor H. R. Mackintosh and Professor A. E. Taylor. Their instant sympathetic response gave me the encouragement I needed to approach others; and to my great delight I found that most, too, readily agreed to help. Gradually the questions and answers began to accumulate, and feeling that they were too good to keep to ourselves, I then approached the Oxford University Press who, seeing their worth, agreed to publish them. The book's reception was quite surprising and it quickly went into nine impressions, four in its first year, and it also led to more questions being sent to me from all sources, not least from Headmasters and School Chaplains from many different parts of the United Kingdom and many from Overseas.

A second series followed in 1938 which went into seven impressions, and a third in 1950; and in 1953 it was decided to make a *Selection* from the three series. (In 1943 a similar book was published called *Soldiers Also Asked* consisting of questions asked by those in H.M. Forces at Padres' Hours and was reprinted the following year.)

Visits to a large number of schools and my connection particularly with three schools in Edinburgh — Fettes College, Loretto School and Edinburgh Academy — made me and many others realize the need now for a completely new series; and the schools themselves, largely through the Headmasters or Chaplains, sent in lists of questions that the boys or girls were actually asking; and here I would especially like to express my gratitude not only to the above schools, but to schools as varied in distance and composition as Eton, Felsted, Lancing, Rossall, Sedbergh, Sherborne, Wellington, and Winchester, and a number of Grammar and Comprehensive Schools throughout the country.

Many of the questions were understandably much the same, and these have, as far as possible, been covered in a comprehensive question; some were of such a contemporary nature as would quickly date them; by no means all were those asked by the original Club boys, and indeed there are some which in those days would never have crossed their mind — who, for example, would have thought of asking questions like 'When are we dead?' (See pages 41—48 of this volume) of questions on outer space and the permissive society (See pages 18—22 and 102—106). All the questioners were anonymous so that the questioners were free to ask what they liked, and all are genuine.

And it is surely right that we should ask questions. Were not the disciples themselves 'desirous to ask him'[1] and Fr. Arthur Stanton of Holborn once said 'we are poor children crying for the light; but it is because we are children and we are alive that we long to ask the questions. Dead men never ask questions. It is because you are alive and your soul is alive and your heart is alive, . . . that you long to know that which is above and about you'.[2]

If this book has shown nothing else to me, it has shown that young people today are even more interested and concerned about belief and the meaning of life than were their fathers.

Each generation to some is never as good as the one before. Youth in one form or another is always 'revolting'. The criticism of young people today is much the same as it ever was . . . 'The world is passing through troubled times. The young people of today think of nothing but themselves. They have no reverence for parents and old age. They are impatient of restraint. They talk as if they alone knew everything, and what passes with us as wisdom is foolishness to them. As for the girls, they are immodest and unwomanly in speech, behaviour and dress.' But 'the young people of today' referred to are those in the year 1294, for the above was written by Peter the Monk! Or this as another example: 'I cannot suppose thee to be such a stranger in England as to be ignorant of the general complaint concerning the decay of the power of godliness, and more especially of the great corruption of youth. Wherever thou goest, thou wilt hear men crying out of bad children and bad servants; whereas indeed the source of the mischief must be sought a little higher: it is bad parents and bad masters that make bad children and bad servants; and we cannot blame so much their untowardness, as our own negligence in their education.' That was written by Mr. Thomas Manton in a prefatory letter to the Confession of Faith in 1643.

These quotations — and I could add others — have a strange contemporary ring about them. The 'good old days' exist largely in older people's imagination when summer holidays were always sunny; but personally I believe that far more true of today's generation are the words of Mr. Anthony Chenevix-Trench, the former Headmaster of Eton and now Headmaster of Fettes, who has said that 'the new generation is morally braver, more truthful, more serious, intelligent, candid and frank'. Bad news is so often 'good news' and the minority hit the headlines. We hear about the fifty students who break into a building but not about the nine thousand nine hundred and fifty who are getting on with their work; but it is the vast majority, so often forgotten, that 'maintain the fabric of the world'.[3] It is of course true that 'the young people of today' have in a moral and spiritual, though not in a material sense, a more difficult world to contend with than was the case when even the first series of *Asking Them Questions* appeared. They are faced with much more publicity — through radio, television and press; they have a greater opportunity for travel and certainly more 'freedom', and though there have always been temptations, for which we should be grateful — for without temptation character cannot be tested — the temptations today can be much more subtle and insidious, and many are such as were unknown a generation ago. But the eternal truths remain and with them still

> . . . those obstinate questionings
> Of sense and outward things[4]

though, of course, some of the 'outward things' of today have a rather different connotation from that which they had to Wordsworth.

There is one point that I mentioned in the Preface to the original series which I should like to underline again, and that is

that no amount of knowledge about religion will ever make a man
religious. To know about our Lord Jesus Christ is not the same
thing as to know him.[5] Yet, is it not almost impossible to know
anyone unless we know something about him? And no amount of
argument can ever by itself convince a man. As Dr. Edwyn Bevan
has so truly said, 'Argument, generally speaking in religion, can
do no more than clear the track; it cannot make the engine
move'.[6] But this is no reason for not helping to 'clear the track'.
Faith, of course, there must ever be, and without it our religion is
worth little. But the word 'faith', if we are not careful, can often
become just another name for laziness; and the clever should not
be confused with the wise. As Professor A. E. Taylor once put it,
'For all of us, the journey will have to begin with a venture of
faith reaching out in a true humility of spirit to things which are
not seen. Nor is this reasonable humility of mind to be disparaged
as what our latest unlovely jargon calls "wishful thinking". For
genuine "wishful thinking" we must turn to the kind of
"agnostic" who "in the dark that covers" him blusters about his
own "unconquerable soul", not to the Christian who says "not as
though we were sufficient of ourselves . . . our sufficiency is of
God".'[7] Our Lord studied the Scriptures, and as we have seen,
asked questions. Dare we do less than follow his example? And
can we do more than pray that his Spirit may be given to us as we
earnestly seek after the truth, so that we may day by day, in our
journey through life, try to become more like him?

Not all the papers included in this book are easy to
understand; some require careful thought and help from older
people; but it is not a bad thing for a young person to find that
truth is not always easily comprehensible;[8] many things may be
seen 'through a glass darkly':[9]

> . . . a man's reach should exceed his grasp,
> Or what's a heaven for?[10]

In other words, this book will never make a man a believer in
the Christian faith and life against his will; but I do think it may
help to clear away some of the stumbling blocks and show that
the Christian belief, when tested by reason and tried out in life,
will prove it is valid and is such that we may reasonably put trust
in it.

I am grateful to Bishop Hugh Montefiore for permission to
include his article and those by the Archbishop of Canterbury,
Bishop Butler, and the Rev. H. A. Williams, which I have, by
permission of the authors, adapted and edited, and the main

content of which formed the basis of sermons preached by them at Great St. Mary's, the University Church, Cambridge, while he was Vicar. And finally I would like to thank all those who have made this book possible by contributing so willingly and so ably. Of the first series, only seven of the forty contributors are, as I write, still alive; and, a generation later, though so many of the questions are basically still the same, the approach differs. Each contributor is of course responsible for his own contribution only and none would claim to give the final word, but each at least, I hope, can set us thinking and talking and so get clearer the truth we are all seeking. And I should like to thank, too, all those others for the great help they have given — the Headmasters and Chaplains already referred to, Mr. N. J. Wheatley, who has compiled the Index, and also The Rev. Hugh Mackay, and my secretary Mrs. Taylor; but I am especially grateful to Mrs. Joan White and Mr. Geoffrey Hunt of the Oxford University Press for their never-failing help, advice and encouragement.

In the first series, the work of forty contributors could be included in one handy volume, because the contributions though coming from eminent men were relatively short and simple, as was then required to meet the needs of the questioners. In this New Series, the ground covered by young people's questions is at least as wide as before, and in order to meet difficulties fully and fairly, the contributors have been given rather more scope. The work was planned as a whole, but for the convenience of readers it is published in two volumes. Part I, already published, comprises questions on the great fundamental subjects like the existence and goodness of God, the inspiration of the Bible, miracles, Jesus Christ, his birth, passion and resurrection, and the life after death. Here, in Part II, will be found questions concerning the Holy Spirit, the Church, the earthly life of the individual and society, and particularly problems of the modern world. Details of the contents of Part I are given for reference on pages 129-130 of this volume and the two Parts are intended to complement each other. The Index of Contributors (pages 131—5) cover both Parts.

Canongate   RONALD SELBY WRIGHT
Edinburgh
Easter 1972

---

1   St. John 16:19.
2   *Faithful Stewardship* by Fr. Stanton (p. 73).
3   Ecclesiasticus 38:34 (AV has 'state of the world').

4   William Wordsworth, 'Intimations of Immortality'.
5   cf. St. John 5:39: 'You study the Scriptures . . . and yet you refuse to
    come to me for life!' (Jerusalem Bible).
6   Edwyn Bevan, *Hellenism and Christianity*.
7   A. E. Taylor, *Does God Exist?* (p. 171f)
8   I am indebted to the late Dr. A. F. L. Smith, then the oldest Fellow of
    All Souls and a former Rector of the Edinburgh Academy, for
    reminding me of a sentence from the late A. J. Balfour: 'A religion that
    is small enough for our understanding is not great enough for our need'.
9   I Corinthians 13:12 (or 'a dim reflection in a mirror', Jerusalem Bible).
10 Robert Browning: 'Andrea del Sarto'.

Contents

xiv

What is Man?

A story is told of the German philosopher Schopenhauer, that one day he was sitting lost in philosophical meditation on a bench in one of the Berlin parks. A park attendant, afraid that this strange-looking individual might be an anarchist plotting a bomb outrage, asked him to produce his papers of identity, or at least to tell him who he was. To which Schopenhauer replied, 'I wish to God I knew.' This question of identity is part of our human predicament. To find some kind of an answer is part of the process of growing up. The psychotherapists can help some of us to acknowledge and realize more fully our identity. The currently fashionable Existentialist philosophy works with the concepts of 'inauthentic' and 'authentic' existence, and the search for authenticity is one of its leading motifs. Some people seem to be able to avoid the question 'What meaning, if any, has my life?', but we feel that the man who has at least asked it is a more truly human being than the man who has never bothered his head with it. Other living creatures seem to have the nature of their species as it were stamped upon them. Man alone seems to be an individual in the full sense; his existence, as Heidegger says, is always his own, and not exchangeable with that of anyone else. He is a willing, deciding, being; in part, at least, he has to create himself, to write his own history. He is one whose task is to find himself. As Chesterton put it, it is good sense to say to a man 'Be a man!' But no one ever thought of telling an elephant to be an elephant. So the question 'What is man?' and the closely related question 'Who am I?' are two crucial questions demanding an answer.

'What is man?' — the question comes, of course, from the Psalms, from the eighth Psalm. But in this, its original context, it is not asked in sheer doubt or puzzlement. The writer believes that he knows. He speaks in wonder and gratitude of what he knows. The knowledge was not won by his own efforts, it was given to him. He is speaking to God, and he says:

> When I look at the heavens, the work of thy fingers,
> the moon and the stars which thou hast established;
> what is man that thou art mindful of him,
> and the son of man that thou dost care for him?
> Yet thou hast made him little less than God,
> and dost crown him with glory and honour.
> Thou hast given him dominion over the works of thy hands;
> thou hast put all things under his feet . . .
> O Lord, our Lord,
> How majestic is thy name in all the earth!

Looking up into the depths of the heavens on a night of moon
and stars this man is almost overwhelmed by the greatness of God
and his own littleness; and yet, God has stooped down to make
man great, and given him dominion over the world and all created
things in it. In this link with God, who has put out his hand to
touch him, and in this delegated dominion over the created
world, the psalmist finds his answer to the question, 'What is
man?'

How did the Old Testament men learn these things? They were
convinced that they had been taught them by events that had
occurred in their own history. They believed that in these things
One had approached them who was not to be confused with
nature, or with themselves, or with the nature-gods of the
surrounding nations. He had shown himself to be the Lord of
both man and nature.

When I was a boy, one used to see among the knick-knacks of
Victorian drawing-rooms articles called stereoscopes. There were
postcards, with two pictures on each, side by side. You fitted
these cards on to a portable stand, and looked at them through a
magnifying pair of spectacles fitted on the stand. These lenses
could be slid up and down a groove until the picture came into
focus. When you got the focus sharp, the effect was almost
magical. You were now no longer looking at a flat picture, but a
three-dimensional one, for foreground, middle-distance, and
background were seen in depth. (The same effect is obtained
nowadays with miniature colour-transparencies set in a cardboard
disc which is placed in a small plastic viewer. To the naked eye
the pictures are flat and unimpressive, but seen through the
viewer they are vivid and three-dimensional.)

Now the men of the lands surrounding Israel, with their
nature-religions, saw God, or the gods, man, and nature, all as it

were blurred and unfocussed, and on one plane. Everything was capricious and uncanny, and in order to help himself man tried to achieve unity with nature and the divine through various mystical, magical, and sexual rituals, by means of which he could help, or compel, nature and the gods to give him good fortune and good harvests. But now there came on the scene the Hebrew people, whose God, they claimed, could not be confused with man, or with nature, for he was the Lord of both. He was not capricious, but true; that is, he could be trusted to keep his word. Gradually the confused picture of things became clear and three-dimensional. If God was, so to speak, above nature, man too, in his lesser degree, was raised above nature. And yet nature, man, and God were not left out of relationship to each other. For God was Lord both of nature and of man, and man had a relationship both to God above him, and to nature below him. It must be understood that this language is figurative, and has nothing to do with the old bugbear of the three-decker universe, which caused so much trouble to the Victorians! It was now seen that man owed loving, obedient response to God in all his life. And man was given dominion over nature, but not absolute dominion, for he was answerable to God for the use he made of it. Though God was no longer confused with nature, yet his glory shone through it, and it praised him in its beauty and mystery, and under man's dominion, if that were rightly used, nature, like man, could be transfigured and praise God as it was meant to do. So man was God's junior partner in history, and steward over a world no longer terrifying, but rational, though full of mystery.

The rest of what I have to say will deal with man in his relation to God above him, and to the world below him, over which he exercises this dominion, and with his fellow-man, who like him is both linked with God, and akin to God, and for whom therefore he is profoundly responsible to God as he is for the world over which he is the subordinate ruler.

The whole Bible is of course full of indirect teaching about man, but this teaching is in the broad sense consistent with itself, and under the limitations of space in the present essay I shall have to confine myself to one important representative concept, which is found both in the Old Testament and in the New, the concept of man's existence in the image and likeness of God. We find this several times in the first few chapters of Genesis, and we do not need to take literally the story of man's creation in the space of a week, to be able to find in this teaching about the image a profound truth. For more than two thousand years there has been endless discussion about the exact meaning which these words could have had for the writer, and the exact meaning that they should have for us, but I think that today few would disagree with the following summary: 'Here the Old Testament writer is describing a likeness or similarity or bond between man and God which is not shared by the animal world or inanimate things. It is not a physical likeness to God, for the author lived in too sophisticated a world to think of God in literally physical terms. In this phrase there is no intention to contrast the image and the likeness; it is as if the writer had said "In the image, that is to say, the likeness". And further, the image is not something that has been obliterated by the presence of sin in the world, for in Genesis 9, verse 6, the writer tells us that God has forbidden man to murder, because his fellow-man is also created in the image and likeness of God. So, even in a world where murder is possible, God will judge the man who murderously sheds the blood of another man made in God's image'.

When you turn to the New Testament, you find that an important change has taken place. The same phrase 'image of God' occurs in the New Testament, and a good deal more often than in the Old. And there are one or two passages where it seems to have the same meaning that it bears in the Old Testament – denoting a dignity in man not shared by the animals, a spiritual bond or likeness between man and God which occurs wherever men are to be found. (See James 3:9, and a passage where this view is implied, though not mentioned in so many words, Mark 12:16–17).

But what appeared to be static and motionless in the Old Testament, has in general in the New Testament been swept into rapid and dynamic movement. There is a point where the deep waters at the head of Loch Awe seem, though they are not, to be motionless, for the surface is often so calm as to mirror the mountains above. But, as one approaches the defile of the Pass of Brander, there are first seen slight stirrings and dimplings of the placid surface, then more and more disturbance becomes visible, until at last the whole river Awe is rushing down in broken commotion towards the salt waters of Loch Etive. Thus in the New Testament the concept of the image of God in man has been brought into powerful and directed movement. The image and likeness of God has now become a divine destiny and purpose for man. Man – every man – has been made in the image and likeness of God – this is the meaning and purpose of human existence. And this destiny has been both made possible and revealed in the life and death and resurrection of Jesus, who is the image of God *par excellence*. That Jesus is the essentially human man is not all that is to be said about him, because in him God has come to meet and rescue men in their journey through history. But Jesus is also the really human man, in whom the central lineaments of humanity have been seen. This is what man was meant to be, this is what God purposes for men everywhere, a fully human existence, to be worked out by each in the special circumstances of his own individual life. And when we ask what this truly human life consists in, we find that it is a life of sonship, trust, and obedience to the Father, and of love to other human beings. This is what Dietrich Bonhoeffer meant when he spoke about Jesus as 'the man for other men' — and it is this destiny for which we were all created.

It may be worth our while to pause here for a moment and ask how far this conception of man tallies with other descriptions which have been offered. It is obvious that a great deal can be said about man that leaves God out of account. Each of the sciences has much to tell us about him; he is a configuration of atoms and molecules in space-time, he is a composition of various complicated chemical substances, he is a vertebrate, and a placental mammal, and Freud and Marx have much of importance to tell us about him. But the claim that we are here making is that, until this relationship to God and his fellows has been acknowledged, what is in some ways the most important thing about man has not been stated.

Further descriptions of man have been given; he is a tool-making animal, and here a characteristic which finds expression in his dominion over nature is touched on. He is the humorous animal, the reflective or rational animal, the one who is not only conscious, but conscious of himself. All these capacities point to man's power to distinguish himself, his interests and concerns, from the immediate flow and urge of instinct; man has a power of standing apart from himself, he can think, plan and decide with a freedom that they do not have. It is not surprising in view of this power of reason that Boethius in the sixth century described man as an individual substance of a rational nature.

But the question is whether even from a philosophical point of view these definitions, true though they are, go deep enough. Reason itself implies not only the existence of an objective and intelligible world, but of other people whose testimony we can compare with our own. Reason itself involves a society of persons. Further, the dynamic psychology seems to confirm the fact that man is a being whose health of outlook depends on his capacity to go out beyond himself, and find objectivity, not only in relation to the world around him, but in relation to other people. In order to achieve this maturity it is important to have had the right relations with other people from our childhood. If we were then given tolerant, understanding affection, with enough discipline to help us to find our identity, then it is easier for us to attain to rationality and objectivity in our attitude to life and other people. Thus dynamic psychology would seem to confirm that even our rationality is not just a mater of individual intellect, but is a profoundly social thing, that we are responsive and responsible beings, that in the end we attain the fullest fruition of our nature in love, and that this is the deepest thing in one sense that can be said of human nature. Here everyday wisdom seems so far to corroborate the Bible view.

We come now to deal with man's power over the inanimate and animate world of nature of which the Old Testament speaks so emphatically. The increase of this power through technological advance has become so incredibly rapid that humanity seems almost to have moved into a new dimension. It is not only the speed of scientific advance, but the constant acceleration in this speed, that is the decisive factor. In former days scientific discovery and invention were on the whole the achievements of gifted individuals. As W.S. Robertson says, 'Because it is a systematic process you can put not just one brain to work on an invention but 10 or 100 or 1000 brains working in parallel. So you get H-Bombs and travel to the moon almost on request.' Whatever Bonhoeffer may have meant by his phrase 'man's coming of age', it is certain that this enormous increase in man's mastery of the world is a part of it. Many things that a few years ago were beyond man's dreams are today in his power, although our language has not yet caught up with the reality and we still say, 'I could no more do that than fly', or 'He is asking for the moon.' And so many situations where only recently all that man could do was to pray, are now under his control to change by his actions. It is as if man had been given a new coming-of-age present, the key of the house of the earth.

The temptation then arises to suggest that 'the religious ideas and usages of the Bible, even the idea of a God who is other than man, must be given up. Man has come of age, and has no need of the idea of God to help him to deal with his own environment' (Lesslie Newbigin). And there are people, of whom Lesslie Newbigin is not one, who deal with this situation in a cock-a-hoop manner, saying, 'We no longer need to pray about the crops or ask a God to take away our headache. We simply fertilize the ground or take a couple of aspirins. In short man will soon be able to do the things this omnipotent God was supposed to do. We will play God.'

It is clear that if this point of view were to prevail, there would result a new conception of man and history from which God has simply disappeared. History will then no longer be considered as a dialogue between God and man, a dialogue of challenge and response. It will have become a human monologue. The holders of this view suggest that the picture of God we have given inevitably leads to infantilism, and that if man is to grow up, he will have to make a unilateral declaration of independence from God. God is here pictured as a vampire-like figure, sucking the blood of man's freedom, and all that is conceded to God is, as Feuerbach put it, filched from man. To be more precise, this view would suggest that the God whom we have been worshipping is essentially an illusion and projection of our infantile desires and fears.

Now it cannot be denied that some of our Christianity has had this infantile character, and in so far as that is true, a reaction against it is wholesome. One good example of such infantilism appeared in the correspondence columns of the *Scotsman* in March 1964. The subject of the letter was the nuclear weapon, and the correspondent actually urged that *instead* of using other means to counter its spread, Christians should resort to the all-powerful method of prayer, pointing out the spiritual satisfaction they would experience in doing so.

In fact, both action and prayer are necessary, but in these days when the scope of our freedom to act has been so increased, it is very important to see that prayer does not become a sentimental substitute for actions that are within our power.

It would also be wise to remember that the notion of man's dominion over nature came into existence along with the revelation of the God who speaks through history, and will hold man accountable to him for his use of this power. It would be reasonable to assume that, if torn out of this context, the conception of man's dominion over nature could lead to the tyranny of a few men over the whole of humanity. The enormous possibilities given us by modern technology should be regarded as a gift, with great possibilities of good, but with equally great possibilities of evil. In the use of them men are faced with an almost overwhelming responsibility, and, however adult they may be, they are deluded if they think that from this point they can 'go it alone'.

The Letter to the Hebrews starts by speaking of the greatness of the Christian faith, and the grave responsibility of those who deliberately reject it. And the writer takes up the words of Psalm 8 with which we began. He is speaking, like the psalm, of the glory and greatness of man, and his dominion. He then goes on to say that this prediction has not yet been fulfilled for men in general, but it has been fulfilled in Jesus. But the glory that he now has is to be shared with humanity, because what he experienced and suffered was not for himself alone, but for us also. This is the final answer to the question about man's nature. We get it from looking at the figure of Jesus. As Karl Barth wrote: 'Who is man? He is one who because of Jesus, can dare to lift his head in hope.'

DAVID CAIRNS

What is the point of prayer and worship and what difference does it make to everyday living?

If you read St. Luke's gospel with your eyes open, one of the things which will strike you is the way in which St. Luke insists on the fact that our Lord prayed often and long. It is when he is praying after his baptism that the Holy Spirit comes down upon him in the form of a dove and his Father announces 'Thou art my Beloved Son; with thee I am well pleased.' When the crowds flocked to hear Jesus preach and to be cured of their diseases because they have heard of his great miracles, Jesus 'withdrew to the wilderness and prayed' (Luke 5:16). The night before our Lord calls his twelve apostles he spends in prayer (Luke 6:12). It is after some time spent in solitary prayer that he asks the disciples, 'Who do the people say that I am?' (Luke 9:18). Our Lord is transfigured on the mountain when he takes Peter and John and James up with him to *pray* (Luke 9:28). Our Lord teaches his disciples the Lord's Prayer when they ask him 'Lord teach us to pray'; but what prompts them to make this request is the sight they have had of Jesus *praying* himself (Luke 11:1). And we are all familiar with our Lord's agonized prayer in the garden, when his tension was so great that 'his sweat became like great drops of blood falling down upon the ground' (Luke 22:44).

Why did Jesus spend so much time in prayer? I am sure it is not the right answer to say that he did so in order to teach us a lesson. We must not think of Jesus as one who lived his life in continual tranquillity, insulated from the doubts and fears and needs of human existence, going through the motions of a complete human life simply to give us an example. Of course he was God; but his human life was a real human life and he experienced the human emotions and felt the human needs. 'For we have not a high priest who is unable to sympathize with our weaknesses, but one who in every respect has been tempted as we are, yet without sinning' (Heb. 4:15). We can be sure then, that Jesus prayed because he needed to pray. He needed to pray because prayer is a duty we owe to God as well as a source from which we draw strength.

The Gospels are full of lessons in prayer. We are to ask our Father with childlike confidence for what we need. If a boy says 'Daddy, I'm hungry. Will you give me some bread?', his father doesn't say 'Ha Ha, son! Here's a stone. Chew that.' And if the boy says 'Daddy, give me a fish', his father won't play a joke on him and give him a snake instead. 'If you then, who are evil, know how to give good gifts to your children, how much more will your Father who is in heaven give good things to those who ask him?' (Matt. 7:11). 'Whatever you ask in prayer, believe that you receive it, and you will' (Mark 11:23—24). And this is true even if you pray for a mountain to move. If at first our prayers are not answered, we must keep on at God, worrying him, one might almost say, like a man knocking up his neighbour in the middle of the night asking to be lent some bread; his neighbour is bound to give it to him in the end in order to be allowed to sleep (Luke 11:5—10). Or we should be like a widow who can't get justice from a crooked magistrate, but keeps on nagging away at him until for the sake of peace and quiet he gives her what she wants (Luke 18:1—5). At the risk of painting a misleading and unflattering portrait of our heavenly Father, our Lord in these vivid little parables reminds us that we must almost pester God in our prayer. St. Paul too gives the demanding advice to 'pray at all times', 'pray constantly, give thanks in all circumstances' (Eph. 6:18; 1 Thess. 5:17—18).

For we owe God prayer. The typical attitude of the Christian is one of loving adoration of his heavenly Father. This is the meaning of the first part of the prayer our Lord taught us: 'Hallowed by thy name, thy kingdom come, thy will be done'. We are not our own masters. God made us out of nothing; he holds us in being every moment of our lives and guides us in his wise providence. It could be frightening and dangerous to be so completely at the mercy of another. But not so with our Father; we are glad to acknowledge our complete dependence upon him because we trust in his goodness. Karl Marx thought that this was a servile attitude of mind, unworthy of the dignity of man. But it is not undignified to acknowledge how much you depend on others. How many men in public life are glad to be able to say: 'I owe all my success to my wife. If it hadn't been for her constant encouragement and inspiration I would never have got where I am today.'

There is a lot of talk nowadays about concentrating on the 'horizontal' rather than the 'vertical' in religion. It was all right, we are told, in less sophisticated ages to direct our thoughts up to a mighty Creator above us; but this way of thinking doesn't help us now. What we must do is to seek God at our own level in our neighbour, like Christ himself, who was 'the man for others'. But this picture is a distortion both of the mind of Christ and of the general human situation. Christ was first and foremost one whose food was to do with his Father's will (John 4:34); he is 'sent' by his Father (John 20:21). The mission he is sent on is to save his fellow men (the horizontal); but he can only do this by doing it for his Father (the vertical). The same, therefore, ought to be true of us. The second commandment, to love our neighbour, implies the first and greatest, to love God (Matt. 22:37—39). It may be that some of us are no longer helped by thinking of God as in any sense above us; we may prefer to think of him within us and among us. But whether we think of him as above us or within us, he is still our Father and Creator, and we still owe him love, adoration and thanks.

Of course, we don't adore and worship God because he needs our adoration. He is not like an actor or sportsman who thirsts for recognition and applause. God is complete and happy on his own, alone in the family of the Trinity. He didn't create us because he wanted admirers or slaves or a hobby. He made us because he is generous, because he wanted to share. So it can't be for his own sake that he wants our adoration; he wants us to worship him because it is for our own good. If we do not adore God we are failing to recognise a basic truth about our lives; there is a dimension missing in our existence. As so often an illustration is to hand in family life; it is not for her own sake that a mother wants the children to say 'Thank you' when she gives them something; she insists on this courtesy because it is good for the child. Karl Marx got it quite wrong; I am less of a man if I fail to adore God.

But someone is bound to say: 'How can it be for my good that I have to worship God when I can see my prayer doing me no good whatever? Prayer is just boring and distracting. The words mean nothing to me.' I shall have more to say about dry and distracted prayer in a minute. For the time being I will simply say that we need to express our adoration of God at least by trying to express it. To try to adore is to adore. I may feel that my prayer isn't doing me any good. If I were left to work things out for myself I might feel that worship was a waste of time. But I know our Lord said 'Pray then like this: Our Father who art in Heaven, hallowed be thy Name' (Matt. 6:9). This is enough to convince me that it must be right for me to try to adore my Father in prayer.

Of course this relationship that we have with God is a very strange one. We need to tell him that we adore him, that we thank him, that we love him, knowing all the time that it doesn't make any difference to him at all. We say these things for our own sake, because we can't get our relations right with him unless we do. After all, when we tell somebody that we are sorry or when we say 'Thank you', we are saying these things not only for the other person's sake but for our own. We *need* to acknowledge that we have been in the wrong, we *need* to express our thanks, though of course the other person wants to hear us say these things too. But in our relationship with God we need to say the things to him but he doesn't need to hear. He doesn't *need* to hear but he *wants* to hear, because it is for our good.

We don't pray in order to tell God things that he doesn't know. 'Your Father knows what you need before you ask him' (Matt. 6:8). Of course many of the prayers we use do sound as if they were designed to tell God things about himself that he didn't know before, like all those prayers that begin 'O God who', and go on apparently to remind God of his benefactions to the human race. But the information-content of a prayer is there, of course, not for God's sake but for ours. It is meant to help us to recall our proper attitude to God, which is one of gratitude for his favours. It is the attitude itself, in fact, which is prayer rather than the words. The words are there just to help me put myself in the right attitude. It is something like kissing someone who is asleep on the forehead and saying 'Goodnight, darling.' Of course, God does hear us. But the point of our words in prayer is that they express what we feel about God or help us to feel what we want to feel about God. You kiss a person not only because you want to *show* them that you love them, but because you want to show yourself that you love them. If a man never kisses his wife, his marriage will soon be on the rocks, not only because he won't be telling her that he loves her, but because he won't be feeling that he loves her. Our lives will not be truly Christian lives if we do not regularly experience the loving adoration of God that is prayer.

There is of course another reason why we pray in words: there is no other practical way in which we can pray together. When the Society of Friends come together for a meeting, for some of the time they pray together in silence; but still for part of the time they will be praying out loud so that all can share the same thoughts about God. Although Jesus told his disciples to pray in secret — 'When you pray, go into your room and shut the door and pray to your Father who is in secret' (Matt. 6:6) — he also told them to pray together — 'When two or three are gathered in my name, there am I in the midst of them' (Matt. 18:20).

But why is it not sufficient for a Christian to pray in private? Because the New Testament shows that we are not to be individual followers of Christ; that all his followers are to be united in following him. We are the branches that go to make up the vine; the limbs that make up a body; the stones that make up a temple; we are God's people of the new covenant; we are in other words members of Christ's Church. One of the characteristic Christian virtues mentioned in the New Testament is 'fellowship' or 'sharing'. All this fits in very well with human nature; for we are not so many individuals, like independent atoms; on the contrary, a person is one who makes and needs to make relationships with other persons. As the Greek philosopher put it, man is a political or social animal. We need one another. And in our prayer too we need one another. Prayer is being in Christ's presence. We are promised that Christ will be present with us when two or three are gathered together in his name. Prayer and fellowship, then, proceed hand in hand. By praying together we grow in unity; our unity helps our prayer to progress, jerking it out of any narrow self-centred rut.

Of course we need to pray in private too, or else there is a danger that our communal prayer will lack depth. Each age has its own peculiar difficulties in prayer. In some other ages the emphasis has been too much on the individual, so that the corporate dimension of prayer was under-emphasized. In our time the danger seems to be quite the opposite: most of us take the need for fellowship so much for granted that we tend to forget that prayer needs sometimes to be an intimate, personal contact with the Lord. It is only by private prayer that we learn to hear God's 'still, small voice'; without it our Christianity, however generous, can be shallow and insensitive.

So far I have spoken about adoration and worship and thanksgiving, but in fact most of what our Lord has to say about prayer in the Gospels is concerned with prayer of petition, when we ask God for things. Some people are very reluctant to pray in this way. They feel it selfish to ask God for favours for themselves; some people even feel uneasy about asking favours for other people. Yet we do constantly need God's help; and even though we know we are certain to receive it, it is still good to ask.

Parents train a child to ask and to say 'Please' when it wants another slice of bread and butter, even though they are sure to let him have it anyway. In this way you train the child to be grateful; you remind him that he can't take it for granted that he is the centre of the universe, but that he has to remember that there are other persons too. When Jesus told us to be like little children, he must have been thinking of this unselfconscious recognition of our complete dependence on God.

So when we ask God for favours we are not telling him something about our needs that he does not already know. Our Heavenly Father knows that we need all these things (Matt. 6:32). Nor do we normally ask for a miraculous intervention by God, a disturbance of the normal process of nature. When we pray for a safe journey by air, we do not expect God to go round miraculously tightening up screws which careless mechanics have left loose; we are rather asking God for something which he has probably already achieved, such as the technical skill and care of the mechanic who knows which screws to tighten, and is too careful to leave them loose. God knows from all eternity that I am to pray for a safe flight, and my prayer is one of the factors that he takes into consideration in his providential guidance of the whole of human history.

But we can't help having the niggling suspicion that prayer doesn't really make any difference at all; that even if I hadn't prayed for a safe journey God would have arranged that the mechanic in his skill saw that the plane was airworthy. We may be willing to grant that when we ask for grace, say for generosity or courage, our prayer does make a difference, if only because to ask sincerely makes us more receptive of the grace for which we are asking. But is the same true of more material favours? I expect most of us have had experiences of cases in which our prayer for such favours seems to have been answered quite spectacularly, but I am sure this is not what usually happens. I remember reading of a man who tried to prove scientifically that prayer did make a difference. He took two similar plants and over one of them prayed repeatedly that it would grow, but left the other to its own devices. As far as I remember he claimed that this experiment proved that prayer made a difference to the plant's growth. But I can't believe that prayer works in this way; it is not a way of commanding God's services to tighten up screws or to fertilize plants. When we pray we are asking a person a favour; and people don't normally do us a favour if they suspect that we are simply trying to discover how they are going to react. We can't *prove* that prayer makes a difference; what we do know is that Christ told us that if we asked we would receive, and that he used to ask his Father for what he needed.

But it is of course true that sometimes when we ask we do not receive what we ask for. It may be that we don't ask hard enough or often enough; our Lord's parables remind us that we mustn't give up too soon. But sometimes we really do try; we ask God again and again, and with all the faith that we are capable of, but still our prayer seems to be no use. The reason is that God will never give us something second-best even if we ask for it. If we pray that someone may recover speedily from an illness, when really it's better for them to go on suffering a little longer so as to learn perhaps to be patient and unselfish, or so as to make other people get on without them, then God will take our prayer as a prayer for what is best for the person concerned and will act accordingly. God is never like the father whose son asks for a Christmas present that they can't afford. The only thing the father can do is to buy the next best thing. With God it is just the other way round; if we ask for the next best thing, God won't be content with this; he wants to give us nothing but the best. He is not a father who spoils us and gives us everything that we want. He is a father who loves us so much that he will not insult us by giving us something unworthy. In this case Father really does know best. And so whenever we pray for something we should always conclude our prayer with our Lord's words, 'nevertheless, not my will but thine be done'. Or if we don't actually say this, at least we should understand it.

We owe God, then, adoration, worship, thanks, apologies; we must make our requests to him. But we should not regard ourselves as people who pray to God from a distance. Above all we are his adopted children (Rom. 8:15–17; 1 John 3:1), we are members of Christ's body (Eph. 4:15–16; 5:30), we share God's own nature (2 Pet. 1:4). God actually lives within us (John 14:23); we contain within ourselves Christ's life (John 15:4; Gal. 2:20). Therefore we can talk to God as one of his family; since our Father has given us the same Holy Spirit, the same loving gift that he gave his Son, we may now join with Jesus in praying, 'Abba', which means not simply 'Father', but rather 'Dad' (Gal. 4:6). We are not any longer members of a different caste, who can only speak when we are spoken to. We can approach God with confidence (Heb. 4:16; 10:19). This is what prayer is: we are at home with God and can talk to him.

But we don't need to talk to him in words. We all learn to pray in words, but the words are not important. There are many ways of praying. Some people pray by turning a prayer-wheel; others by reciting the same little prayer over and over again in a way which seems almost mechanical; others by passing a string of beads through their fingers while the same words keep passing through their mind; others like praying by singing hymns; others express their prayer with incense and genuflections and other grand ceremonies. But all of these ways of praying are only helps to prayer; they are not prayer itself. I am reminded of the question young people sometimes ask: 'Is sexual intercourse the same as love?' I suppose the answer is that intercourse is a way of expressing love, but it is not love itself; there can be intercourse without love, and love without intercourse. So too, all these ways of praying are simply helps to prayer, but are not prayer itself. I can perform them without praying; and I can pray without performing any of them. Prayer is simply a meeting with God, when we raise up our mind and hearts to him, and we can do this without words or without actions. In fact, this may be what God is trying to teach us when we find that we don't seem to be able to pray at all. We are in danger of mistaking the words and the actions for prayer; so he has to teach us that prayer isn't any of these things, any more than love is intercourse. If we want to pray and try to pray then we are praying, even if our minds don't seem to be on God at all. 'Seek and you shall find'; to try to pray is to pray. If we can learn to keep on trying even though words seem pointless and our minds seem blank or far away, we are beginning to learn what prayer really is.

If we can organize ourselves well enough to be able to spend a few minutes every day in prayer to our Father who is in secret, this must make a great difference to our lives. Even the silence and recollection itself has great value. We know Wordworth's complaint of the way in which the bustle of life prevents us from seeing the meaning behind the details and blunts our spiritual powers.

> The world is too much with us; late and soon,
> Getting and spending, we lay waste our powers.

If we can stand away from the trees we are more likely to be able to see the wood. Only the wood is God; and we can hope to see him, not in the detached way in which we admire scenery, but only in the personal loving contact that is prayer.

Prayer, then, should give us a sense of perspective in life; we are able to see things in relation to God. Prayer, too, should strengthen in us the motivation we need in order to live unselfish lives. It is easy to love those who are lovable, but no one appears lovable all the time. These times when love is hard are the moments for which we need the strength of prayer — the strength that Jesus himself sought in the Garden of Gethsemane before his Passion.

EDWARD YARNOLD, S.J.

*Have not new discoveries, e.g., in space,
brought a new responsibility and challenge to
the Church?*

I will begin with a quotation from the second book of Esdras[1]
'And I said, O Lord, thou spakest from the beginning of the
creation, even the first day, and saidst thus; Let heaven and earth
be made; and thy word was a perfect work. And then was the
spirit, and darkness and silence were on every side; the sound of
man's voice was not yet formed.'

The second book of Esdras enjoyed wide popularity during the
early centuries of the Christian era. The original text was Greek,
but at least five other versions are known. We can therefore
assume with some reason that the writer's account of the creation
enjoyed the same type of popularity as the account of the
modern astronomer does today. Today we are possessed of
marvellous devices for the exploration of space, great optical and
radio telescopes, and space probes. The power which these
instruments give us tends to imbue our statements with an
arrogance which ill becomes mortals set amid the grandeur of the
cosmos. Indeed, our statements sometimes tend to imply that we
can soon look forward to a completely scientific account of the
processes by which the cosmos was created.

I am going to suggest to you that this is not the case and that,
in fact, there is little advantage in our present description of the
beginning of the universe over that provided by the writer of my
text so many centuries ago.

Of course it is undeniable that during the last few decades our
instruments have enabled us to formulate a wonderful and
exciting description of the universe. Gone, for ever, are the old
ideas that the earth on which we live is the centre of all existence.
Indeed, the geocentric view of our place in the universe was long
in dying. Three and a half centuries ago the belief that the Earth
was fixed in majesty at the centre of the universe with the sun
and the stars revolving around it, became untenable. However, in
spite of the increasing powers of man's telescopes it needed
another three centuries before the evidence was produced to
show that the sun and the solar system were not at the centre of

the universe. For all that time the modification of man's outlook regarding his place in the cosmos required only minor adjustment compared with the revelations of our own lifetime.

Many of us here have lived in an epoch during which a few privileged astronomers have been given the powers to tear aside the curtains which have hindered our understanding of the immensity of the cosmos. Now we know that the Milky Way which is such a splendid sight in the night sky is a Galaxy of one hundred thousand million stars. Our home in space — the earth — is a planet of the sun, which is an average star of this galaxy. We are far from the centre of this system, right out in one of the spiral arms in which the stars are arranged. In our daily life we are rushing through space as the galaxy rotates, unaware of our motion and without power to influence or control our astronomical future.

If we are a microcosm in the Milky Way then the Milky Way itself is a microcosm of the universe. For, wherever we look in space our telescopes reveal countless similar galaxies of stars distributed with a high degree of large-scale uniformity. The regions of space and time in which we see these galaxies are almost beyond normal comprehension. Those of us who use radio telescopes think nothing of turning our instruments on to a galaxy as a daily routine in order to record signals which left the galaxy five thousand million years ago. These radio signals have been travelling through space with the speed of light, 186,000 miles per second, for 5,000 million years. Our knowledge of these distant regions is a knowledge of time past - we look back five thousand million years into the past history of the universe — into an epoch before our own earth came into existence. Within these regions of space and time there are many thousands of millions of galaxies containing vast numbers of stars like our own Milky Way.

Our description of the universe is indeed more impressive than that given in the book of Esdras and every day that passes finds more detail added to our picture. It is when we probe into the first causes that our confidence weakens — when we ask how this vast system of stars and galaxies came into existence.

This problem is beset by the most fantastic difficulties. For example, I have just mentioned that our knowledge of the universe lies in the past. As we penetrate deeper into space so we move back in time. The light from the great nebula in Andromeda has been 2 million years on its journey towards us and it brings us knowledge of the nebula, not as it exists today, but as it was 2

million years ago when the light left the nebula. As the power of
our instruments has increased during the last few decades so
knowledge of earlier and earlier epochs of the universe has
become available. With each new accession of power we have
expected to find signs of some change in the past history of the
universe. But this has not happened. Today we can study with
relative ease the condition of space and its contents as it was five
thousand million years ago, but as far as we can see the universe
has been changeless on the large structural scale over this
immense span of time.

At this moment those of us who are working with radio
telescopes are struggling with the further extension of another
few thousand million years into the past, and the question
whether this additional penetration will reveal signs of change is a
matter of contemporary dispute. Our observations of these
distant regions reveal a strange state of affairs. We find that space
is expanding and that we are separating from these distant
galaxies at enormous speeds. Moreover the further we penetrate
into space the greater is the speed of this expansion until at our
present limits of penetration of five thousand million light years
we are separating from the galaxies at a speed of 86,000 miles a
second, nearly half the velocity of light. Every minute we recede
from these galaxies by more than 5 million miles.

I think that although there will be a further deepening in our
understanding of the universe we cannot even postulate a
situation which will enable us to evade the barrier with which
nature seems destined to protect the observation of the initial
processes. We may describe it, as we believe it to be, either in
simple language like the writer of Esdras, or in the complex
equations of the modern theorist, but as far as the precise
description of the creation of the universe is concerned I do not
think it possible that our descendants two millennia hence will
see much fundamental difference in the accounts in the popular
works of the first or twentieth century.

I think, also, that we do well to remember that almost all our
knowledge of the epoch we are discussing is speculative and
theoretical — as it always has been. After all, our ability to make
actual observations of distant regions of space is a recently
acquired facility. The beginnings of this movement in the early
part of the seventeenth century were violently opposed by the
Church because Galileo with his telescope produced observational
evidence that the Earth was not the majestic centre of the
universe. Galileo's ideas and his telescope survived to lead to a

great scientific revolution. Commentators often compare the break-through in our own age with that made three centuries ago. The analogy is a good one and we are indeed fortunate to have lived through the drama involving the telescopes, sputniks and space probes of the last few years. Unfortunately the analogy is good also in a most sinister sense, because events take place today which may hinder, or even destroy, our ability to continue the advance in our astronomical observations. Indeed it is not by any means inconceivable that the great progress in our observational studies of the universe from Earth may turn out to be a limited interlude in the history of man — limited that is to a period of a few centuries beginning in the seventeenth and ending in the twentieth or twenty-first centuries.

My anxiety about this matter arises because of the lack of control on the activities of man in outer space. The Sputnik and its immediate successors and the landings on the Moon seem to be the precursors of a brilliant new era of scientific progress. Alas, in so short a time many things have been carried out by scientists in the name of science which really have little to do with true research. As a result, space is now in process of contamination with many thousands of objects and although the effects are at present scarcely discernible, the proliferation of this orbiting debris over a few decades may have grave efforts on our ability to penetrate to the remote parts of the universe. Furthermore, space rockets are now beginning to approach our neighbouring planets in the solar system on which it cannot yet be excluded that some form of developing organisms might exist. The Christian ethic is interpreted to govern our life on earth. It is a matter of urgency that we should consider our attitude to these experiments which might involve the contamination of other abodes of life forms. There may be others in the universe for whom this planet is their heaven.

With these modern devices man also possesses the power to make atomic explosions in outer space. Scientific use was made of this ability some years ago when small atomic explosions were made at a height of a few hundred miles in order to investigate certain features of the earth's environment. Unfortunately in the summer of 1962 there was an extrapolation of this experiment involving a high-yield nuclear device which has had a most serious effect on the possibility of certain scientific investigations. The spirit and outlook with which the event was staged was most grievous. I have referred to the arrogant outlook which our modern scientific tools sometimes generated, and nowhere is this better illustrated than in this matter of the high-altitude explosion. The event was justified both before and after, by scientists in the name of science, who gave their authority to predictions which turned out to be quite wrong.

When I was a young man I was horrified that the Church had attempted to stifle the advance of science by the persecution of Galileo, and I felt thankful that in the succeeding centuries the conflict had been partially resolved. Now I am not so sure that we have reasons to be thankful. At least at that time the Church was able to fight effectively from the basis of its own edicts. Now it has lost most of that power, because its leaders have failed to interpret the Christian ethic in a developing and dynamic sense in the face of the incredible advance of our material powers.

It is a tragedy of our time that the Church which in past ages exerted such a stabilizing effect on man, is now so preoccupied with the minor adjustments of its ethics to daily life, that it remains blind to the vast responsibility with which it is faced as a result of our recent scientific progress. In *The Pilgrim's Progress*, John Bunyan describes how the Interpreter showed Christian the man who was so preoccupied with raking to himself the straws, the small sticks and dust of the floor, that he did not look up or regard the One who stood over him with a celestial crown. It would be hard to imagine a better simile to illustrate my argument, for those who cry out for religion to give new guidance would do well to turn their gaze to the stars and consider for a while their cosmic responsibilities.

The words with which St. Paul charged the Ephesians are more appropriate and urgent today than they have ever been. 'Put on all the armour which God provides, so that you may be able to stand firm against the devices of the devil. For our fight is not against human foes, but against cosmic powers, against the authorities and potentates of this dark world, against the superhuman forces of evil in the heavens.'

BERNARD LOVELL.

---

[1]   2 Esdras 6:38–9 (in the Apocrypha).

What is the essence of Christianity?

'What is the essence of Christianity', Or to put it in a form which is more appropriate to the current mood of suspicion of large-scale commitments: 'How little can I believe and still call myself a Christian?'

If this question had been asked a generation or so ago, the popular answer would have been, 'It is sufficient to believe in the fatherhood of God and the brotherhood of man', and many people would have rested content with it. Today, they are so confused and distrustful about the first part of the answer that they would be very doubtful about agreeing to it, and yet some of them would still like to claim a Christian name. Like many other liberally-minded people who are not Christians, Bertrand Russell among them, they would probably prefer in these days to speak of the primacy of love rather than use the old-fashioned phrase, 'the brotherhood of man', but to that they would hold fast. They would go on to see as the distinctively Christian element in their belief their relation of commitment to and solidarity with the figure of Jesus Christ, the supreme exemplification of 'the man for others'. They would want to say that they understand 'love', which is otherwise a very generalized word, in his terms and that they want to live together in his way. They might recognize that the further belief in 'the fatherhood of God' may have had a supportive value for men in previous ages but they do not feel the same need for it themselves and cannot see convincing evidence which justifies it, so that they prefer to remain agnostic.

No-one would deny that, just as Socialism is 'about equality', so Christianity is 'about love'. Yet it is not mere dogmatism or conservatism which makes most Christians believe that a distinctively Christian profession must mean more than this. If to be a Christian means having a special relation to Jesus Christ, then it is hard to see how one can avoid making a decision about what was central in his teaching and his life, his conviction concerning the source and the goal of love. If Christianity is 'about love' in

Jesus's terms, it must also be 'about God' and about his relation to man.

This is the point of the confession of faith which those admitted to membership of the Church were asked to make in the earliest days of Christianity. They were asked to say, 'Jesus is Lord', and we could paraphrase it in words like these, 'to be a Christian is to believe that the Reality which was present to the people of Israel, whom they believed to be the Creator of all men and the One to whom all men are answerable and whom they called the Lord, is uniquely and decisively present in the man Jesus'. It is his relationship to this Lord which determines the nature of the love which meets us in the man Jesus. It possesses three distinctive qualities which mark out its uniqueness. Its source lies outside ourselves. It can be appropriated only by an act of self-transcendence, which takes us out of our existing selves into a new situation. Our relation to it is decisive for our lives. Without these qualities, it is hard to recognize as Christian love.

The fact that the source of this love lies outside ourselves means that it comes to us as *grace*. This is at the very heart of our apprehension of Christian love. It is not generated by our natural vitality or virtue nor must it be identified with normal human affection, although it may do a great deal to extend, intensify and direct that affection. It comes as a gift to the undeserving, and always with an element of the miraculous about it. This is what encourages the man of Christian faith when he wonders whether he is not deceiving himself in saying that God loves him. He knows that he did not have it in himself to invent the forgiveness and the new power and the new insight into his neighbour's needs which he now possesses. If there were any hint of self-deception about it, it would be unable to have the effect upon him which it has. Having been blind he now sees. He cannot believe that that which gives him the power to see properly can itself be an illusion.

Secondly, this unmerited grace evokes the kind of response which takes us out of ourselves. While it meets us where we are, it does so in order to lead us to a new place, and frequently to a place where previously we should have preferred not to be. There is a sense, of course, in which all outgoing love of others prompts us to transcend ourselves, but the love we meet in Christ has a uniquely radical quality because it makes us see that our ability to love is not in itself enough to justify us. Even our ability to love itself needs to be redeemed. What Christian experience makes us see is that the finest fruits of past love, and these include the fruits of Christ-inspired love as much as any others, can go bad unless those who enjoy them are constantly renewed by the divine initiative. Even the salt of the earth can lose its savour. The trouble with a generalized belief in the fatherhood of God and the brotherhood of man, which lacks this dimension of understanding of the corrupting influence of the world even on love itself, is that it can lead to a further belief in things like 'the neighbourhood of Boston', in the words of an old joke about the American Unitarians. That is to say, it leads to an over-valuation of the cultural fruits of past responses to grace, to complacency about one's present situation and therefore to an inability to venture into the unknown in self-transcending new acts of love. Christian history itself provides many sad examples of such over-valuation, complacency and refusal to venture, with the result that men, refusing to run the risk of losing their life, have not found it. The only hope of avoiding this temptation lies in seeing that God's love can never be identified with human love and always demands a response which takes us out of ourselves.

Thirdly, the love which confronts men in Christ is decisive. There is nothing about which the Gospels are more emphatic than this need for radical decision. This love thrusts responsibility upon us, it demands a choice exercised in freedom and it carries with it an element of finality. This is why those who have known this love often speak of it as terrible. The compulsion which it lays upon us is not that of an overwhelming power which sweeps us aside but that of a personal reality which will not allow us to avoid accepting the burdens of our freedom. It makes us see that in Christ we meet life's authentic meaning and do so in such a way that we have to make up our minds about it.

It is this which prompted the first Christians to affirm the deity of Jesus Christ and to make such bold statements about the cosmic significance of his work. The writers of the letters to the Colossians and the Ephesians had discovered that a great flood of light had been thrown on human existence by Christ and their imaginations were inspired to see the whole universe as the sphere of his victory. They expressed their ideas in the forms of thought of their own time, which are different from ours, and we have to do a great deal of translation in order to grasp their meaning, but it is important for us to see what moved them to such flights and to capture some of its splendour for ourselves. Christian faith was born not only out of a conviction that love was of central importance but that, in Christ, it had proved itself stronger than sin and death and evil. It arose when men received the assurance that the Power in whom Jesus Christ believed had honoured the faith in which he went to the Cross and had enabled them to share that faith. However narrowly we may wish to define it, and however agnostic we may wish to be about the nature of life beyond life on this earth, a belief that an event of more than human significance took place in the resurrection of Christ seems to be of the essence of Christian faith.

In the course of history, Christianity has inevitably gathered around itself beliefs which are not necessarily wrong but which do not speak to the heart of the human condition, or do so in ways which are no longer helpful. This is what makes it important from time to time to raise the question from which we began. Ours may be an age in which a great deal of clearing away has to be done in order that men can discover the Gospel again in its pristine freshness. In the process, much that many people in the past have regarded as essential may have to go. Experience throughout the ages suggests, however, that it is hard to recapture the creative and renewing power which is distinctive of Christian faith unless men see that it is not only 'about love' and 'about Christ' but also about God's victorious love made known in Christ.

DANIEL JENKINS

What is the choice between Christianity and Humanism?

Throughout the history of thought, Humanism has appeared in divers forms. So has Christianity. But there has always been between the two a difference of kind rather than of degree. For Christianity is a religion, Humanism a philosophy; and while the devotees of both of them preach a noble way of life in which man is to serve man, the Humanist's defence of his way of life when challenged about it is a rational defence, based on reason, but the Christian's defence is that and something more, that transcends reason. To the Humanist, of whatever kind, man is the ultimate court of appeal as regards his standards and his conduct. To the Christian, of whatever kind, the ultimate standards and sanctions lie outside and beyond man; and though they can be known in part by reason and deduction, from observing the kind of phenomemon that man *is*, their most sublime nature could not have been known to us without a direct revelation from God incarnate, in the person of Jesus Christ.

The Humanism of the ancient Greeks is perhaps the noblest ever yet. In the *Dialogues* of Plato, and the *Metaphysics* of Aristotle, the ultimate creator is an abstraction: an original First Cause, deduced from the argument that everything is caused by something anterior to it and that there must have been a beginning, uncaused and eternal. Man could attain to some knowledge of this First Cause by the use of his highest power — reason. If on the one hand he personified God — poetically — into indeed the whole family of deities in Greek mythology, on the other hand he could work out logically a code of ethics and conduct derived from studying what men in observable fact are. He could deduce the rights of man (to life and liberty and property) and the duties of men (to his fellows individually, and to society). It is indeed in this way that philosophers since Classical times have elaborated the whole theory of private and public and international relations generally accepted today, in terms of that 'law of nature', or Natural Law, based on what the subject-matter *is*: whereby for example, there must be a fundamental difference of method between *training* an *animal* (whose intellect is *passive* and can *be led*) and *educating* a *person* (whose intellect is *active* and can lead itself).

By the time the second period of Western Humanism began, there had intervened more than a thousand years of Christianity, with its signal change of emphasis as regards the nature and the motivations of man. God, the First Cause, has shown itself as a *Person*: in the Incarnation. Christ said not 'Follow your reason to the end of an abstract argument about the divine', but 'Follow Me'. Truth was no longer just a conclusion from propositions, but a way of life in terms of them. This is what Sir Richard Livingstone meant when he said, in setting the Christian life over against the Greek humanist life, 'Evil will vanish more quickly from a world in which sin is regarded as an offence against God than from one in which it is regarded as missing the mark.'

The highest in man, as taught by Christ and the Apostles, was not reason but love (*caritas*); living is a person-to-person relationship, and its bond (however ill or well accepted) is respect and affection. One could certainly be truthful and kind on grounds of reciprocity; indeed the pre-Christian golden rule already said 'Do as you would be done by'. But there is a world of difference between reciprocity, which is only enlightened self-interest, and the Christian command to love, which was absolute and unconditional: since men are brothers and born of one Father.

The Humanism of the Middle Ages was thus God-centred. The subject of medieval literature was God, whose will was the inspiration and the measure of the saints and heroes. The spires of the cathedrals drew to a point, upwards (as Chesterton reminded us). 'I would rather feel compunction', said Thomas a Kempis, 'than know its definition'. And Thomas Aquinas, just before his death, murmered that his mighty *Summa* of philosophy and Christian theology had but scratched the surface of what was true about the divine. Scoundrels there were too, in plenty, but in perpetrating their evil deeds they did not call them, nor believe them to be, good deeds: lust they knew to be lust, and did not call it the New Morality.

It was during the second of the three periods in which up-to-date thinking has been labelled Humanist that there occurred a change of focus that *could* make such a paraphrase possible: during the two centuries from about 1450. This was a time when the face of the globe was itself changing in spectacular ways. The professions had began to become laicized, the whole of the New World was opened up and penetrated and exploited, the modern sovereign state came into existence, the first breakthrough in educational 'visual aids' (printing) was revolutionizing communication, and Christian unity was sundered by the Reformation.

For many years now, scholars have thought of this period less as 'Renaissance' and more as 'Humanist'. For the element of re-birth (in scholarship and the re-discovery of ancient Greece and Rome) was less than once thought: scholarship had never decayed; and on the other hand 'Humanist' indicates far better the career of the period as it reached and then passed its climax — the study of Man as man, and the study of the Ancient World as a classical example of high perfection in thought and the arts and the sciences and order and government, which must be used as a model and also brought up to date for the service of 'modern' man.

But it is important to bear in mind that the people of the Renaissance did not call *themselves* Humanists when referring to their lines of thought. The word *humanista* was a technical term: it meant in the fifteenth century those scholars who taught certain particular classical texts known as the *studia humanitatis*. And indeed the first 'Renaissance' generations, from Petrarch down to and beyond Thomas More, in no sense over-emphasized the human (as against the divine) in man. These two points have to be insisted on by Christian apologists today whenever Scientific Humanists claim an ideological parentage from the Renaissance. The Humanism of the Renaissance, glorious in its flowering of scholarship and in all the arts, was at first a flowering of Christianity itself. Its highlights, stemming from the Old Faith, are Vittorino and Petrarch in Italy, Colet and More and Elyot in England, Vives in Spain, Erasmus throughout indeed all Europe; and stemming from the new, reformed Protestantism a generation later and onwards, the cult of courtesy, crystallized into the gentleman, as it has come down to us from Bacon and Peacham and Milton and Bunyan.

But this Humanism later lost the all-inclusive sanction of attachment to the divine. Its successors, as currents of thought dominant in their day, were the Rationalisms of the eighteenth-century Enlightenment: the general tendency to 'de-mythologize' which Lecky (in his history of it) rooted in the decline of belief in miracles and in witchcraft; the Deism of the French Encyclopedists and of Voltaire; and the outright claim (going back to the ancient Briton, Pelagius) that man was capable, here on earth and by his own efforts, of reaching perfectibility.

It is part of the Christian critique (Catholic and Protestant) that such fatal deviation from the original norm had been implicit already in the Renaissance itself; that it was inevitable once the centre of attention had shifted, in study and in motivations, from God to Man. Rosalind Murray's *The Good Pagan's Failure*, and Dorothy Sayers's *Begin Here*, are still among the most trenchant studies of this point: the point, as E. J. Hughes put it, in his *The Church and the Liberal Society*, that the shift in the centre of gravity meant that man could henceforth look for the solutions to all his problems only in himself; and that, 'once man is exalted for his humanity, and no longer for his divinity', the end of civilization is in sight.

To the Christian, then, it is not surprising that the full conception of the human person, as biological and economic and psychological and rational and aesthetic *and religious*, has become deformed and fractionized in the Humanisms that have followed. Each of these has stressed one facet of the human person above others, and thereby done violence to the complete, integral conception. The Humanism of Marx was exclusively economic and fundamentally materialist; to Freud, the key that unlocked all the secrets of the personality was psychological; to Julian Huxley it was biological; to one of the greatest and most revered of the modern Humanists, Gilbert Murray, it was (as it had been to the Greeks) rational. All these keys are indeed keys. But none of them is *the* Key. Nor is the religious key the *only* key to the secrets of the personality. They are not revealed till *all* the keys are used simultaneously, neglecting none of them: just as, in the Principality of Andorra today, the seven-lock muniment-chest of the whole polity cannot be opened unless by the seven headmen of the seven districts (each of whom has a key) together.

This is not to say that the Humanism which is in the ascendant today, Scientific Humanism, claims that Science can do everything and solve all man's problems. Perhaps the most lucid (and the most engaging) study of this Scientific Humanism in Britain today is still that of Mrs. Margaret Knight. And its application to the education of the coming generation has been worked out most sensitively and humanely in Lionel Elvin's *Education and Contemporary Society*. Far from being a further 'fractionizing' of the concept of Man, these works make a positive contribution. In a Western World given over to more and more of uncritical materialism, they are steps on the road back to the Christian, integral view.

They should do much to repair the unfortunate 'image' that today's Humanism has in Christian eyes, as created by emphasis in the press. To take but one example of this: Faced with the population 'explosion', and the problem of world-hunger, there are two possible lines of attack: to limit births, and to increase food production and distribution. Christian apologists say that far too much emphasis, in public discussion to date, is on the former of these, with corresponding neglect of the latter; and it is a pity the publicity for bodies like the British Humanist Society has been so much along the negative lines of abortion, divorce and euthanasia.

The philosophy of Scientific Humanism is on a plane far above this. And its leaders rightly insist that the crux of discussion is the relationship between moral values and religious beliefs. Can there be ethics without a theological basis? The question is of passionate interest to the Humanist, dismayed at how the world is slipping ever further into materialism. He feels the urgent need, in a society 'now predominantly secular', to 'develop a code of social responsibility which can form an integral part of education'. And he is eager that in achieving this he can have the active support of Christian allies. 'For working purposes', says Lionel Elvin, 'though not for theoretical discussion, the two positions are by no means impossible to reconcile. If the religious person is speaking with someone that supposed divine law leaves unimpressed, he resorts to arguments from natural law, and, except where some divine law conflicts with what the humanist alleges is demanded by human experience, the two positions are close enough to permit of rational discussion and . . . . a great deal of agreement.' Or as H. J. Blackham has put it, theoretical differences only come in when they lead to differences in policy. The central question theoretically, they recognize, is 'What is the nature of Man?' — but there can be, despite fundamental difference on the answer to this, action in common to save society. For there is common ground, between the philosophers' Absolute *Values* and the Christians' *Dogma* (on the one hand) and the Humanists' conclusions from human *experience* (on the other), as to what sort of *conduct* is desirable and to be fostered. 'Whatever our differing explanations of the sources of our moral values, can we agree enough in practice, on what is right conduct, to give us coherence in our moral educational aims?'

Of course we can. And the educational plane is here the most important plane of all, since in the school (which is an extension of the family) the foundations are being established for adult conduct on the social and all the other planes.

This highly profitable field for joint exploration has now been surveyed in depth in the brochure *Humanism and Christianity — The Common Ground of Moral Education.*[1] The joint group of educationists whose labours produced this *exposé* take the word 'education' to cover 'the *whole* area of experience and study which is provided to assist the moral development of the children', involving specific teaching and pastoral care. Their united witness goes very far, despite the difference of approach. The 'conflicting viewpoints', however, faced squarely at the end, are of course formidable. The Humanist is agnostic or atheist, with no ultimate reality of 'the personal and loving God' to appeal to; evil is not, for him, man-made, but is 'in the nature of things'; *specific* ideas about the nature and character of God have, for him, no place in moral education; man has, *within him* the powers for his own personal and social transformation'; Jesus was totally human; there is no life after death. At bottom, 'Humanists regard the principles of moral behaviour as specifically the outcome of man's moral and religious striving throughout history, whereas Christians, while accepting these formative influences, see in them the eternal revelation of God'.

The reflection in that last quotation is precisely that of an older and more pungent reflection: that the difference between Christianity and Humanism is the difference between a living plant and cut flowers. The mirage of human perfectibility without religious doctrine has been before the eyes of very good men since pre-historic times, when dawning reason led others to appreciate that not all things are what they appear to be. The observation-and-experience basis of modern Humanism is sound enough so far as it goes. By all means let us keep our feet on the ground. But not our head. Experience is only the *basis* of our knowledge (as Aristotle insisted in the days of the very first Humanists). And sound moral conclusions from rational experience do not commonly meet with automatic acceptance in practice. That they *should* do so, is because of what man's nature *is;* and this is something *more* than rational, and more than ordinary observation and reflection. On what constitutes the 'more', the Christian and Humanist differ. There is a gulf between them.

This gulf has nowhere been better explained, nor more compassionately, than in Jacques Maritain's *True Humanism*, first published over thirty years ago. Because of the gulf, all modern Humanism is 'materialized spirituality', against which 'the active materialism of atheism and paganism has the game in its hands'.

There are fundamentally but two Humanisms, one centred on and finding its standards in God (theocentric Humanism), the other centred on and finding its standards in Man himself (anthropocentric Humanism). Ancient Humanism and post-Renaissance Humanism are the latter. They lack a vital element which, going beyond what they truly assert, is *central* to Christian Humanism: namely, the grace of God. True freedom depends upon grace, which is its source. Freedom based on Man's *own* view of his best self will *inevitably* be at the mercy of what particular men may choose to do when they have the power. There has of course been tyranny and denial of freedom by Christians too; history is besmirched with it. The Humanist will always be right in his objection to the Christian, for the Christian will never be at the level of his Christianity. But what is crucial is the difference of levels. There is a world of difference, a difference of kind and not merely of degree, between asserting freedom as the absolute birthright of every human soul, made 'in the image of God' and uniquely valuable in itself, and asserting freedom on grounds that are but the agreed consensus of men and 'accomplished under the sign not of unity but of division'.

That is why the Christian sees ultimately definite limits to his hopes of a working alliance with Humanists today, who hold (at the most) 'humanist truths disfigured by four centuries of anthropocentric humanism', and at some point on the uphill road back from materialism will part company with him and leave the climb to him alone. 'Only a conscience rooted in the Gospel can cure the tragedy of a conscience rooted in naturalism'.

So it comes to this. In the twentieth century beset by a *crescendo* of rank materialisms, from the Marxist and Nazi totalitarianisms to the rampant 'permissiveness' of today, an alliance of Christian and Humanist in action can be something to be thankful for: especially since both are now minorities. To the extent that Humanism's declared way of life is based on that Natural Law which is Christianity's own basis, they *need* each other in their common programmes of humanitarianism, social and educational *action*. But there is a point at which the guidance of the Natural Law stops short, and beyond that point the Christian has to stand alone. The highest thing in man is not reason but love (*caritas*). God is love, and man's highest love is literally the divine spark in him, as in the supreme self-sacrifice of Christ himself.

Beyond the partnership of Christian and Humanist in social

action lies the gulf as regards *why* they act together. It has been re-stated in the 1969 Christmas broadcast of Pope Paul VI:

> What we must tell you on this happy day, sons and
> brothers, is this: without Christ there is no true humanism.
> And we implore God and beg you, men of our time, to spare
> yourselves the fateful experience of a Christ-less
> humanism. A brief reflexion on what the history of yesterday
> and today teaches us would be enough to convince us that
> human virtues, developed without the Christian charisma,
> can degenerate into their contradictory vices. Man, if he
> makes himself a giant, if he spurns a spiritual, Christian
> animation, collapses under his own weight. He lacks the
> moral strength which makes him really a man; he lacks,
> in short, true awareness of himself, of life, of his reasons
> to exist, of his destinies: man, on his own, does not
> know who he is. He lacks the authentic prototype
> of humanity; he creates idols for himself, idols that are
> fragile and sometimes dishonourable. He lacks the true Son
> of Man — Son of God; a living model for the true man.
> True humanism must be Christian. As our first duty.
> As our supreme interest.

A. C. F. BEALES

---

[1] By J. Hemming and Howard Marratt; 1969; from Borough Road College, Isleworth, Middlesex; pp.27.

Has not Christianity been tried and found wanting?

We might begin our answer by considering the first occasion on which people came to the conclusion that the teaching of Jesus had been tried and found wanting. It happened in his own lifetime, and is chronicled in the Gospel according to St. John: 'From that time many of his disciples went back and walked no more with him. Then said Jesus unto the Twelve, "Will ye also go away?" Then Simon Peter answered him, "Lord, to whom shall we go? Thou hast the words of eternal life." '[1] You see, the occasion was a critical one. Jesus had gathered round him a popular following. But he was well aware that the motives that inclined many to accept his leadership were the wrong ones; that few of his disciples understood his purpose and none its implications. So he challenged his followers; and many decided that he was not their man. They left him; and the inner circle of his chosen disciples watched their support dwindle away. No doubt they were uneasy and alarmed; for not only was the tide turning against them; they had heard their leader deliberately courting the disaster. The shadow of defeat fell upon them and chilled their spirits. Jesus felt it, too; he turned to them and asked, 'Well! Are you going, too?' It was, we may say, the first crisis in the history of Christianity, on which the future depended. Simon Peter, the fisherman, decided it; and their hesitation and disappointment can be felt in his answer, 'Lord! to whom shall we go? Thou hast the words of eternal life.'

That was a long time ago — nearly two thousand years. A few months later the defeat had reached its climax. The religious and secular authorities put an end to his preaching: the people he had disappointed hounded him to his death: the inner circle of his disciples forsook him and fled, and Simon Peter, for all his impulsive loyalty, denied with oaths and curses that he had ever known the man. Another rebel against the sacred tradition had been silenced: another disturber of the Roman peace had been finally eliminated. Even to the few who had clung to him in desperation it was the end.

Yet in truth it was only the beginning. It was not the final defeat of a local revolt against authority: it was the most spectacular and significant victory in the annals of human history. This is the plain verdict of the facts. For two years or three, Jesus went about the villages of Palestine speaking to obscure people: then, because what he said seemed dangerous to the authorities, he was put to death. Today, we count history backwards and forwards from him: rightly — for whatever else may be doubtful, and however we may seek to explain it, he had changed the course of history. In a real sense history began with Jesus: not, indeed, the story of the vicissitudes of human experience, the record of the rise and fall of cultures and nations; but history as a continuity of action and purpose, which moves now before our eyes towards the unification of mankind. The living forces which are shaping the destiny of the world have their roots in Christendom; and Christendom, both Eastern and Western, is the creation of the Christian churches. Behind it all, as the seed from which it has grown, is the life and teaching of Jesus.

It may be said that this is to claim too much. Is there any significant sense in which one man can be singled out as pre-eminently the artificer of the destiny of mankind? The very idea is preposterous. At the most we can allow that in course of time Jesus became the central figure in the religion of Europe; and an elaborate ritual and a vast body of mystical doctrine was built round his memory. The fragments of it still linger on among us, but the march of history is flowing beyond them and leaving them behind — the wrecks and relics of an ancient priestcraft. Surely that is all there is to it, if we appeal to history? I think not; I believe that such an account misses the whole point. Even in the life of individuals, what unity and continuity are achieved depend upon an aim clearly perceived and constantly pursued. The continuity of history since Jesus is of this kind. It moves to a goal, more and more clearly envisaged; sustained by transcending motives constantly renewed. The progress which marks the history of Christendom is no process of natural evolution. It is not characteristic of human society as a whole. It depends now, and has always depended, in the last resort, upon men for whom the meaning of their own lives has become the realization of the human brotherhood, in whom the natural motives have been transformed by the vision of a world to be saved by their own sacrifice. It was this vision and this transformation that came into the world with Jesus.

It was no accidental result of his moral teaching. Indeed, Jesus was no moralist — neither Eastern sage nor Greek philosopher. He was a man sent on a mission with a work to do, a task to accomplish. There is nothing of the mystic visionary or the inspired dreamer about him. On the contrary, he is intensely practical and overwhelmingly deliberate. He is sent to proclaim the good news of the coming of the Kingdom of Heaven. That is the purpose of God and therefore the objective for Man — the meaning of human life. Since it is the purpose of God it will be achieved. Since it is the purpose of God, it is in some sense the natural objective of all men. But it is not the actual objective of ordinary living. How then is the real issue to be faced? How can the springs of action in men and women be transformed? The radical transformation of the motives that determine the relationships of men in society to one another — that is the problem as Jesus saw it; and to this his life was devoted. How can man be born again; redeemed from sin; remade into a new creation? That was the question Jesus set for himself and for mankind. He thought of himself as the Sower, sowing the tiny seed that would grow into a great tree and fill the whole earth. The ground had been prepared — so he saw the history that lay behind him. Now he had been sent to sow the seed broadcast that would spring up and grow where it found good soil. He undertook the task; pondered the conditions of accomplishing it; rejected with complete realism all the seductive short-cuts that would prove blind alleys, and fulfilled the conditions with unflinching determination. The 'seed', he said, 'is the Word.' Not the idea in the mind, which has neither hands nor feet, but the living word which is the self-expression of an inner integrity. He realized also the condition of its creativeness. 'Except a corn of wheat fall into the ground and die, it abideth alone.'

This was the task which Jesus took upon himself and to which with full consciousness he limited himself — to sow the seed of the transformation of human motives. If you would ask whether his mission was a success or a failure, you must ask only this question, 'Are there signs, in the centuries that have passed since his mission was complete, that the seed is growing, that it is bearing fruit in the creation of a new spirit in the relations of men, in a transformation of human motives?' No other question is to the point; and to this question the answer is undoubtedly 'Yes'. You can read the answer in the bitterness of his enemies and in the growing fury of their oppositions; in Frederick Nietzsche, for instance. You can hear it in the testimony of a great multitude throughout the ages — and today they are to be found in every nation under the sky — who bear witness to a transformation of the springs of life in themselves. From Paul of Tarsus to the last convert in modern China or Nigeria — men and women of all races and classes and cultures, they talk of him not as a great thinker or sage or moralist — but in strange, intimate terms — as their saviour or their redeemer, as a master who is a friend — as someone who has done for them something so miraculous that they can only express it by worshipping him as the incarnation of the Creator of Heaven and Earth. Of that great cloud of witnesses few have not faced the evidence of defeat and echoed the words of Simon Peter: 'Lord! to whom shall we go? Thou hast the words of eternal life.'

A great company — Yes. But what have they done and what are they doing to save the world? Even if we grant that many have in the past found Christianity a refuge and a consolation for their individual frustrations, what does it all amount to? We are living in a world which walks in the shadow of death. Two world wars have come near to ending the civilization that the Church built up. We look forward with anxiety to an even greater cataclysm; hoping to be saved from it, but without a solid ground for the hope. If ever the world needed salvation it is now. We all know it; though we try not to think about it. Does anyone really think that Christianity can save the world now? We must listen to the growing multitude of honourable, earnest, and thoughtful voices which answer, 'No'. Especially we must attend to the verdict of those — and they are not few — who work and sacrifice to achieve the very brotherhood of man that Jesus proclaimed, and for whom Christianity is at best a blunted instrument and at the worst the centre and symbol of all they fight against.

What do these men say?

They say: 'Christianity is dope. Behind its fine phrases and high sentiments about human brotherhood there is an ugly reality. When has the Church been the leader of the oppressed against their oppressors? Has she not always supported worldly authority, however unjust and extortionate, against those who strove for freedom and justice? She has preached the virtues of poverty while she amassed wealth; inculcated humility while her prelates became a byword for pride. She has fought in the van of the struggle against the freedom of the human spirit, against enlightenment, against science. She has talked peace, and blessed war. When her own power or prestige has been threatened no policy has been too machiavellian, no weapon too inhuman for use in its defence. When she had the power, she tortured and slew all those who dared, for conscience' sake, to oppose her claims. Now that her power is gone, she must use other methods; but at heart she remains the same — the last refuge of superstition, bigotry, obscurantism, and reaction. That is your Church! — a facade of fair words that cover an inward rottenness.'

That is what they say. What is the answer? There is no honest answer except that it is true: that it is not the whole truth does not make it false. Yet it is not surprising; for such has been the predominant character of established religions everywhere and at all times. Neither is it new: the whole diatribe is an echo from the past. You will find it in the twenty-third chapter of St. Matthew's gospel, the verdict of Jesus upon the established religion of his time. The accusations are the same — only the language is different; more passionate, more bitterly contemptuous. To this day the words sting and burn; and the bitterest enemies of religion in our day have never approached the lyrical fury of his denunciation. ('Ye compass sea and land to make one convert; and when he is made ye make him twofold more the child of hell than yourselves . . . Blind guides! which strain at a gnat and swallow a camel! . . . Whited sepulchres . . . outwardly beautiful . . . full of dead men's bones.')

It is a mistake to imagine that the battle for Christianity is a fight between the Church and the world. It goes on both in the Church and in the world. It is no struggle of creeds or of institutions: its battle-ground is in the minds and hearts of men and women. Christianity, in truth, is the impact of Jesus — of his life and teaching — upon the world, and the slow transformation of human motives that is the continuing result of that impact. The Christian Church, even at its worst, has been, and will long remain, the medium through which the story of Jesus and the record of his teaching are kept operative in the world. However she may wrap them up in mysterious philosophy; or render them almost indecipherable with glosses and interpretations; however her acts and policies, her ignorance or her cowardice, may belie her profession; she must perform this service to mankind, or collapse in mockery and derision. No greater service has ever been done by any human organization than this; and upon the fulfilment of this task the salvation of the world depends. If today there are men who labour to realize the human brotherhood, turning their backs on Christianity and building on other foundations — that in itself is evidence of the transformation of human motives and human objectives that has already been made effective: and the standards by which they judge and condemn Christianity are themselves the measure of the Christian influence.

In our time multitudes have turned from Christianity to find other leaders who would offer short cuts to the promised land. They have looked to science and to the techniques that science has made possible. They have turned to political programmes for the reorganization of society. They have put their trust in power. Their power has turned the world into a bedlam; science has given them the atomic bomb; the statesmen move from deadlock to deadlock. One thing at last is so clear that it has become a commonplace. Unless the fear and suspicion that frustrates all efforts to reconcile the nations can be dissipated, the outcome must be a convulsion of the world before which the imagination quails. This is the issue on which everything hangs — the transformation of human motives. This was the issue that Jesus faced, and to which he offered a solution. He began a process which has slowly but surely worked to transform the motives of men in their relations with one another. I know of no other force that operates in the world in this way and to this end. And so — as I see many going away to other leaders or to none, and the shadow of defeat falling upon the Christian cause, I am dismayed and filled with doubts. Yet in spite of everything, I can only stand with Simon Peter. When I hear in my heart the question, 'Will you also go away?', I can only answer as he did, 'Lord, to whom shall we go? Thou hast the words of eternal life.'

JOHN MACMURRAY

[1] John 6:66—8.

When do we die?

Apart from prisoners in the condemned cell it is given to few to know with any precision when they are going to die. We are, perhaps, the happier for our ignorance; but it is very inconvenient. Death is *the* inevitable event in our lives and it usually affects quite a number of persons as well as the central character in the event. If we knew when it is going to occur, we could make so many arrangements to obviate so much inconvenience. It is, however, an inconvenience with which we have learnt, quite literally, to live, and the human race has had a very long time in which to accustom itself to the inconvenience. But of recent years we have been faced with another uncertainty which is more than an inconvenience; it can be a positive embarrassment. We have never known when death will occur; today we quite often do not know when it *does* occur. Our ignorance springs paradoxically from our increased knowledge and our embarrassment from the enormous strides which have been made in medical, surgical and nursing techniques and skills.

Not many years ago, when the heart stopped beating and the breathing ceased, a man was dead, and that was that — or, at least, that is what we thought and everybody was content. Today, the heart which has ceased to beat can be re-started, not once, but several times, and the patient sometimes makes what appears to be a complete recovery and thereafter leads a happy and a useful life for many years. Did that patient die?

The patient whose breathing threatens to fail, and even the patient whose breathing has stopped altogether, can be placed in an iron lung which will perform for him indefinitely all the necessary functions of respiration of which unaided he himself is incapable. Renal failure, fatal when complete, can now be averted by transplanting a kidney from a corpse or from a living donor or the patient can be put on a machine which will perform the functions of the kidneys for him. Even the heart can be transplanted, and the day may not be distant when, sometimes at least, such transplants will achieve what has so far eluded them, a fair measure of success.

If these achievements at present promise no more than the prolongation of life, they also arouse hopes or fears as to what the more distant future may hold in store for us; for, though it seems highly improbable and very undesirable that death will ever be banished, the indefinite postponement of its advent raises appalling problems. The whole social order is thrown out of gear, when the population's rhythm of replacement is upset, and, in an age which is threatened with the population-explosion, the situation could rapidly become acute. Indeed, we already have a foretaste of these problems, brought upon us by what are essentially the same medical skills and springing from our realization that we no longer know when death occurs.

Not long ago a woman wrote to her bishop and, in all seriousness, asked if he could tell her whether her husband was still alive. His body was in fact lying in a bed in the hospital, the object of constant care. But was he alive? Some months before, he had met with an accident and had suffered what was regarded as irreparable injury to the brain. He appeared to be profoundly unconscious and no one saw any prospect of his ever recovering any further measure of consciousness. But his lungs worked and his heart went on beating and his other bodily functions continued. Devoted nursing kept the body in a sanitary condition and supplied it through a tube with food. While there did not seem to be any prospect of his condition's changing for the better, there was also no reason to suppose that it would deteriorate. In such a condition pneumonia often supervenes and, when it does, if left to take its course, it finally removes all doubts, for lungs and heart will soon succumb. But today antibiotics can effectively deal with pneumonia. Should they be given? Of course, if we may conclude that the patient is already dead, not only antibiotics but ordinary nourishment may, and should, be withheld, and then the lungs and heart will quickly stop. But is the patient dead? And, if he is not dead, does it follow that nourishment should still be given and infection kept at bay by antibiotics?

The poor woman's question defeated the bishop. Her problem, however, is by no means a rare one.

A man in the North of England went out for a stroll one evening and had the misfortune to be accosted by a drunken sailor who knocked him down, thereby injuring his skull.[1] He was taken to hospital where an operation was performed, apparently successfully. He did not recover consciousness, but his heart and his lungs continued to function for some fourteen hours while he lay in bed. Then he stopped breathing. He was immediately put on a mechanical respirator. After a further twenty-four hours he was taken to an operating theatre where one of his kidneys was removed and transplanted into the body of another and undoubtedly living patient who required a new kidney, and the artificial respirator was then switched off. As a result, the heart stopped beating and, within a very few minutes at the most, the first patient was undoubtedly dead. But was he alive or dead before the artificial respirator was switched off?

A great deal turns on the answer. The surgeons who had charge of him claimed that he had died when his breathing ceased on the first occasion, fourteen hours after the operation on his head and twenty-four hours before the respirator was stopped. They claimed that the kidney which was transplanted was taken from a mere cadaver and given to a living person. Were they right? If they were right, then responsibility for his death lay at the door of the drunken sailor who had caused the head injury and who, *prima facie*, was in consequence guilty of manslaughter. But, if the surgeons were wrong, if the patient was alive when his kidney was removed, and if his death stemmed from the switching-off of the artificial respirator, then (apart from a possible defence of mistake), some person or persons in the hospital were *prima facie* guilty of murder, while the drunken sailor's criminal responsibility would seem not to have exceeded that for an aggravated assault.

The legal problem was never resolved. At the subsequent inquest the Coroner's jury returned a verdict of manslaughter against the sailor; but in the Magistrates' Court the charge against him was reduced to one of common assault, and, at the Assizes, no evidence was offered on the Coroner's committal. Since the decisions of Coroner's Courts and of Magistrates' Courts are of no value as precedents and since there was no argument at the Assizes and since the responsible persons at the hospital were never prosecuted, we are still without authoritative legal guidance. But this dramatic case highlights the nature of the basic problem with which we are concerned, namely, when, or what, is death?

It does not, however, exhaust the problem, for it does not touch on cases such as that about which the woman wrote to her bishop; it does not touch on those cases where the heart has not failed nor the breathing ceased, but where the patient lies, apparently profoundly unconscious and, so far as can be seen, with no prospect of any measure of improvement. Are such patients alive or dead? Are they to be differentiated from patients, such as the victim of the assault by the sailor, where a vital function has ceased, but has been artificially restored and is being artificially maintained?

Again, a great deal depends on the answer. If the profoundly and irrevocably unconscious patient is in fact dead, our duty towards him has already switched from care of his body to prayer for his soul. If, however, he is still alive, we are faced with another problem. What is our duty towards him? May we attempt to evaluate his life? We can have no doubt that the patient's continued inert existence is a grave encumbrance to others; his body is occupying a bed which is urgently needed by patients for whom the prospects of a cure are hopeful, and the demands which his helpless presence makes upon a numerically insufficient nursing staff are formidable. But may we conclude that his continued existence is of no value to him? And, if we may reach such a conclusion, what follows from it?

Some would say that logically it is justifiable to kill him and that such killing should be called, not murder, but euthanasia. Others, while shrinking from that, would maintain that there is no obligation to do anything to keep such a patient alive and that, by simply refraining from giving him nourishment, the inevitable result will quickly be attained. Yet others would say that the obligation to feed and wash the patient continues; but that there is no obligation to take extraordinary means to prolong his life, and, in the category of extraordinary means, they would place both the artificial respirator and also such common practices as the giving of antibiotics.

Probably most persons would agree that we must now revise our concept of the doctor's duty. It used to be stated that his duty was to preserve life. Today perhaps we can agree that it should be re-stated, and that we should now say that the doctor's (and the nurse's) duty is to do his best for his patient. Very often this will be the preserving of the patient's life; but not always. Where, so far as we can tell, the patient's life is useless even to him, and still more where it is a positive burden to him, as in the case of a painful terminal illness, the doctor may be doing his best for the patient by not prolonging the process of dying. When, then, pneumonia supervenes, the doctor will not combat it by giving antibiotics; he will rather relieve the patient of pain and will let him slip away peacefully and with dignity.

It may be said that the problem of evaluating life, implicit in the problem of the doctor's duty, is a different one from our main problem which is concerned with when and what is death. The two, however, are closely linked. We have seen something of the difficulty of deciding when death occurs. We have seen that it cannot be solved simply by looking to the cessation of certain bodily functions. We have not as yet seen what other criterion is to be applied. Perhaps we are approaching the problem from the wrong angle. Perhaps we should be asking, not *What is death?*, but *What is life?* What is life? When does it begin? When does it end? It is an urgent and current problem and it has been and is prominent in the controversy concerning the ethics of abortion.

When does human life begin? There are three theories which at times have found favour; at conception, at quickening, and at birth.

Of these three, quickening is probably the least tenable. There is no reason to suppose that anything significant happens to the foetus at this moment; it is no more than the moment at which the mother becomes acutely aware of the living organism which she is carrying. Yet it is a moment to which importance has been attached, fostered perhaps by the account in St. Luke's Gospel[2] of the visit of the Mother of the Lord to the Mother of the Baptist, wherein it is related that, when the Baptist's Mother saw Our Lady, 'the babe leaped in her womb.' It is a moment which has been of legal significance, for a woman could not be hanged if she was quick with child, the test being whether she was quick and not whether she was pregnant.

Birth, of course, is a moment of great significance and has been recognized as such. The law recognizes it as a necessary prelude to murder, in that in order to establish murder, it is necessary to show that the birth of a child preceded its death, thus differentiating the crime from abortion where the death precedes the birth. Subconsciously, too, most persons probably tend to date the beginning of their existence from the moment of birth.

Most probably the strongest claim can be made for the moment of conception. It is the moment when, due to the fusion of two separate entities, biologically something completely new comes into existence. While it does not as yet have a separate existence and, until birth, is dependent on the life of the mother, it does have an existence and, even if it is not yet a human being, it is potentially one. It is its importance as such which gives rise to the opposition to the legalizing of abortion.

To recognize the importance of the foetus is not necessarily to claim, as some theologians do, that the moment of conception is the moment when a soul informs a human body. Underlying such a claim is implicit the idea that a sharp dichotomy can be made between soul and body and almost suggests that somehow, somewhere, there is a ready-made soul waiting to be popped into a convenient body. Whatever be the origin of the soul, may it not be that soul and body grow together?

We can but speculate. But, on this line of speculation, it is possible to conceive of a gradual development of soul and body which at some point reaches a high degree of integration. It is an integration which can be snapped by sudden death, or it can gradually lessen as the bodily functions decline until a peaceful death at a ripe old age effects a complete separation. At that point we know what happens to the body; not only do the bodily functions cease, but the body, left to itself, disintegrates in the process which we call corruption. We do not all share the same certainty regarding the fate of the soul. Some, of course, deny its existence. Others deny its continued existence after the death of the body. The Christian, with others, believes in its survival of bodily death and makes the further claim that death opens the door to what can be a fuller life. These are matters of great importance, but not ones on which we can enter here. We began with the problem of what and when is death. Having in mind that death is the negation, or, at least, the end, of life, we have been forced to ask the question, *What is life?* Its definition has not been attempted and there is much about its nature which eludes us, notably its genesis in any individual case. But perhaps some sort of picture is gradually emerging. It is the picture of a progress or of a constantly moving process from a small beginning up to an optimum and then into a decline.

If this be a true picture, then death is not necessarily at any well defined moment. It itself is a progress or a process and could even be said to begin at the moment of the inception of life, whether that moment be the moment of birth or of conception; we begin to die the moment we are born. 'Life is an incurable disease', as Abraham Cowley wrote, and 'In the midst of life we are in death' as the Book of Common Prayer puts it, both statements being made from the material viewpoint. The converse, from the non-material viewpoint, is St. Paul's statement[3] that 'to be spiritually minded is life and peace', which imports the idea that not merely birth, but the whole of life, is a traumatic experience leading to a second and more spiritual birth at death.

If, then, the true picture is that death is a progress which cannot be expressed in terms of a single moment, it still remains true that for practical purposes we need to be able to identify a moment as the point in time where we draw the line, the point of no-return. Where is it to be? It can no longer be for all purposes the cessation of heart-beats and of breathing, for we have seen that these are no longer conclusive and that, with modern techniques, they do not necessarily mark the point of no-return. For these reasons the modern tendency has been to concentrate on consciousness. When the electroencephalogram is flat for an arbitrarily chosen length of time, there is a tendency to say that the damage to the brain, whether from accident or lack of oxygen, is irreparable, and from that to make the diagnosis that consciousness has gone and the prognosis that it will never return. From that it is but a short step to equating this condition with death. There are dangers in this, for diagnosis, and, still more, prognosis, can be wrong. But danger is probably inevitable and we shall have done all that we can if we take reasonable precautions to minimize the risk of mistake.

If we do decide to adopt this approach to the problem, we shall find that a certainty, proved to be false, concerning the moment and fact of death is replaced by a cautious fluidity. With the continued advance of medical and surgical techniques, both diagnostic and therapeutic, we shall find that the moment when it is safe to pronounce a man to be dead (for that is the practical problem) will vary from time to time. Some claim that the responsibility is that of the doctor. This is to claim too much for him and to lay too much upon him. We are all concerned in the problem and it impinges heavily on the lawyer and the theologian. Because we are all concerned, we must try to reach a consensus as to the criterion to be applied in deciding whether a man is dead. In so doing the guidance of the medical profession is of enormous importance; but the conclusion must, if possible, be the conclusion of us all. Once a criterion, however variable, has been established, the special responsibility of the doctor arises. It is he who must say in any given case whether the criterion applies. It is he who must say whether the point of no-return has been reached by the patient. It is the point of no-return which will vary from age to age according to the state of medical knowledge and skills. The argument here suggested is that, for practical purposes, a man may be pronounced dead when he passes the point from which no medical skills, current at the time, can bring him back, and when there is no reasonable prospect of the situation's changing by reason of medical advances.

This approach rests largely on a concept of life which equates it with either consciousness or potential consciousness, and acute embarrassment will still be caused by the profoundly and apparently irrevocably unconscious patient whose bodily functions have not yet failed. In such cases caution alone will make those responsible very slow to pronounce life extinct. But, even if life is not extinct, the life, so far as we can judge, is one without either actual or potential value, even to the patient. If life is still there at all, it is kept ticking over only by such assiduous and arduous care that it scarcely lies in our mouths to make the demand for it. Even the strictest theologian may conclude that in such cases the purpose of the patient's earthly existence has been fulfilled to the limit of his capacity and that, if his soul be tied to his body, the time has come, in the patient's interests, to let the knot dissolve.

Does this make sense? It is advanced very tentatively. Does it make sense both practically and theologically? Unless it satisfies both practical and theological criteria, it should be rejected. Is there anything which makes better sense?

> There's nothing certain in man's life but this:
> That he must lose it,

wrote Owen Meredith[4]

> To everything there is a season, and a time to
> every purpose under the heaven; a time to be born,
> and a time to die,

wrote the author of Ecclesiastes.[5]

The attempt to distinguish the seasons is the task with which we are now confronted.

                                                    E. GARTH MOORE

---

[1]   See the *British Medical Journal* (1963), No. 5353, p.394.
[2]   Luke 1:39—45.
[3]   Romans 8:6.
[4]   *Clytemnestra*, pt. xx.
[5]   Eccles. 2:1—2.

Where is heaven nowadays? And if it is nowhere, how do we get there?

It is great fun writing about heaven, and I have written a book about it.[1] Today is just the sort of day to be writing more briefly on this delightful subject, and to be trying to think out with you the question whether the pleasantness of the idea can have any foundation in reality.

Today is a gloomy December day and my wife is upstairs in bed with 'flu. While my children are at school I sit down and begin thinking about death. I am helped to brood on the grimness of our fate by an incident which happened a few days ago. I am not now thinking of the road accident which happened a few yards away, resulting in a woman's death. I did not know the victim, and modern civilization has become a place where average people like me, without imagination or compassion, take many thousands of road accidents every year for granted, just as we expect to see death on television and in the newspaper every day. No, what I am thinking about is on the one hand something which has affected one personally, and is on the other hand something which is really less tragic than a fatal accident.

I am thinking about what happened to a television programme of Handel's *Messiah* which the B.B.C. made in King's College Chapel, Cambridge, when I was Dean of King's. The programme was made with great care; some of the best singers in the country came as soloists; our choir was kept at it day after day, as bit after bit was filmed and filmed again in order to get everything perfect; and the total cost to the B.B.C. was, I am told, about £18,000. The result of all this work was shown on the B.B.C. 2 channel, but the plan was to get a really large audience for *Messiah* by repeating the programme on the Sunday after Christmas this year in the main TV channel, B.B.C. 1. The video-tape of the programme — the only one in existence — was sent to an engineer for a last-minute check, to make sure that no defect in the tape would spoil this great audience's enjoyment. He put the video-tape in the machine. There is on the machine a button which in a matter of seconds erases every sound and sight, so that the video-tape can be used again. The engineer, doing what he thought he had been asked to do, pressed the button. In the words of a headline reporting the incident,

Hallelujah — That was!

This disaster was little enough in comparison with the accidents, or in comparison with the murders, or in comparison with the wars, or in comparison with the 'terminal illnesses' which keep the mortality rate at one hundred per cent. But pressing the button to obliterate *Messiah* was, to my mind, an act which encourages thought, for not only do insignificant people like us die; the best that exists is doomed to share in the universal death, whether or not another star collides into our earth before it becomes uninhabitable, and whether or not an American or Russian or Chinese statesman orders the pressing of the button for the nuclear end of civilization. You and I are not in fact as immortal as we may think we are when young and fit — but what matters more is that the whole of existence is under the button. All of art is; all of morality is; every human hope is. Brecht said that the man who is laughing is the one who has not yet been told the news.

You can see now, if you did not see at once, why today I enjoy thinking about heaven; about a life beyond the reach of a lorry on the road; about a music which cannot be destroyed; about a glory more powerful than death. But is it true?

There has recently been a good deal of talk about what nonsense it is to think of heaven 'above the bright blue sky'. But what exactly is involved in such an idea?

The picture of God as a man living above us, and out of our sight, and beyond all the universe — that is a picture which comes naturally when we worship. Countless people in the past have used that picture, and anyone who worships God finds that the picture comes naturally today. Because the human mind does think in pictures — look inside your own mind and see! And if you are to have a picture, what is the alternative to this one? Are we to picture God as an abstract design or as a splurge, less interesting than a face? Are we to picture God as beneath us, like the worms in the earth? Are we to picture God as just like us so that he becomes 'one of us' and nothing more? Are we to picture God as confined to the universe, its prisoner? I suggest that a moment's reflection shows why this picture of God as a man above us, out of our sight, beyond the whole creation, forms in the mind of the worshipper. But recent discussion has rightly insisted that this picture of God can be badly misleading. It can suggest that God is remote from us. To say that he is in 'a country far beyond the stars', as a poem does, may be to suggest that he never gets nearer (although no Christian poet has ever made that suggestion). That is why we have heard so many protests against locating heaven miles away. We want to think about God as near.

Ah, but this is not the main challenge which is offered nowadays to belief in heaven. Anyone who thinks about what it means to worship God (in the Jewish, Christian, and Muslim tradition at any rate) can easily see that religious believers believe in a God who is *both* personal *and* more than that; *both* high above us *and* deep inside us; *both* out of our sight *and* closer than our own breathing; *both* more tremendous than the universe *and* the power that keeps the universe in existence. We need both the love and the majesty, both the height and the depth, both the invisible and the friendly, both the Creator and the Spirit. But the main challenge is to the validity of this belief itself. Does the belief stand up to examination? Does it make any sort of sense to believe in a God who can't be pinned down in one place? The men going to the moon did not pass God's house. The men probing the unconscious depths of the mind of man need not worry that they will disturb God. But does that prove that God does not exist? Thoughtful people who believe in God have a way — very irritating to the atheist — of saying that God is, 'not there, not there' or 'not that, not that'. Does that mean that they are talking utter nonsense? Or is religious language, with all its difficulties, the reflection of an experience?

There is a special word for the experience which is at the heart of religion: the word *ecstasy*. Derived from Greek, it means literally 'standing outside'. It refers to our moments of great wonder, when we are so struck by the beauty or greatness or lovableness of something or someone that in sheer excitement and pure joy we seem to be standing outside our normal little lives. This condition, or something very like it, can be brought on by drugs; but it can also occur without any kind of artificial stimulus. The classic description of it in a young man's life is in Wordsworth's poetry, specially his *Prelude*; but 'ecstasy' is not restricted to the poets, or to the well-known mystics, for many people have had this experience. Have you not had it? Or at least, do you not respect people who claim to have had it? Atheists can experience ecstasy, and many have said that they do. But many millions of people have believed, and do believe today, that such experiences are clues to the reality of something or someone beyond (as well as within) the universe. For in those moments we feel intensely that reality, the way things are, is after all friendly; and we are after all part of that reality. In those moments of ecstasy, we say 'My God!' And there have been so many people who have claimed to have experienced God in this way — or who at least have respected others who made that claim — that belief in 'something more', something 'transcendent' (to use the technical term), has often been regarded as part of what makes a man human. The conclusion has been drawn that man is a religious animal.

Religion is a vast affair which is based on this experience of ecstasy. Religious art is the attempt to recapture something of the feeling, and Handel's *Messiah* is the attempt to sing about it. Prayer is the attempt to remain in touch with God, and theology is the attempt to speak honestly and intelligently about religion and about religion's claim to have met God. Once you grasp how religion begins in ecstasy, you can begin to make sense of the phrases which you find linked with the idea of God. You will, for example, often come across the word 'almighty'. This refers to God as not controlled by anyone or anything. Another common word is 'perfect'. This means that God is not subject to any mental or moral weakness. Another word is 'infinite'. The idea is that God is not limited in space. Another word is 'eternal'. This refers to God as not restricted by time. We have to make pictures of God, drawing on a tradition (for example, the Christian tradition). These pictures inevitably use ideas that God is in space (so that he is pictured as like a man, for example), or that God is in time (so that he is pictured as doing something). But although we have to use such pictures, we also have to modify or even abandon them if we are to worship God as almighty, perfect, infinite, and eternal. For the reality of the transcendent God, experienced in ecstasy, must be beyond any limit. He, who is more real than anything we can know anywhere, must be no-thing, and he must be no-where. He is not a member of any class of objects; nor is he a member of any class of people; and even to say that he 'exists' is an understatement.

I have been writing about 'God', not 'heaven'. This is deliberate. The word 'heaven' is a traditional word meaning 'life with God'. People while they have used pictures of God have also developed pictures to suggest a little of what life with God, when you are not God yourself, must be like. You know the common pictures. *White clothes* suggest purity (like a bride's wedding dress). *Gold* suggests something very precious (like an engagement ring). *Harps* suggest that the happiness of life with God is more like music than it is like chatter (and do we not sing hymns when people marry?) *Wings* suggest that there is now no limitation on humanity. Man is not confined to the earth, any more than God is. (Don't lovers talk in such terms, at least before he and she find that marriage means work? 'It begins when you sink into his arms, and it ends with your arms in the sink.') If these traditional pictures or phrases do not help you, invent others. Remember that every picture or phrase is suitable up to a point, if only it hints at the unutterable glory of God.

But here we are — and how do we get there? Here am I, and for all I know when I go out this afternoon I may be killed on my bicycle, and for all I know this essay may be burned accidentally before it is printed. What does heaven really mean to me? Here are you, wondering. 'It all sounds very fine,' you say to yourself, 'but isn't it all airy-fairy?' And you are inclined to turn away from thoughts of God and heaven, back to what you can touch and see.

Let me try to state, very briefly, what I *don't* believe about how we 'get to heaven'. For it may well be that you are thinking that one of the ideas which I reject is what I mean by 'heaven'.

First, I *don't* believe that heaven is 'pie in the sky when you die'. That is, I don't believe that heaven is a duplicate world, a copy of this one only better, which we enter when we leave this world. I don't believe that white or gold or harps or wings should be treated as more than pictures in this connection; the reality of heaven, to my mind, depends solely on the reality of the almighty, perfect, infinite, and eternal God. Take God away from heaven, and heaven would cease to exist in any sense at all. (I am not worried because Spiritualists often produce reports of heaven looking like a holiday camp, with no God in sight. I think that there is something in Spiritualism, a reality which they are getting at; but I believe that eternal life is a great deal more special, more mysterious, than the materialistic trivialities which Spiritualists often produce with the good intention of comforting the bereaved.)

I don't believe that heaven is 'the opium of the people'. That is, I don't believe that the hope of heaven is a drug to take people's minds off their present miseries. Of course thinking about God, which I am doing now, is a cheerful business. But to talk about heaven while cheating people of their rights on earth is a great sin, often denounced in the Bible and in the scriptures of other religions; and to escape from this life's duties by religious sentimentality is also a sin, although no doubt a pardonable one when people feel very miserable. Belief in God, and in God's purpose for us, ought to make us cheerfully active. The lives of the real saints show this.

I *don't* believe that 'everyone automatically goes to heaven'. That is, I don't believe that God totally ignores what we decide, what we think and do and say. On the contrary, God respects our free will. In this life God lets people think and do and speak against him, and it is conceivable that God would allow someone to defy him, and to reject his love, to the bitter end. That shows how much value God attaches to human freedom. What we think and do and say therefore matters, for we ourselves have a share in shaping our habits and characters. Thus we have a share in shaping our destinies in eternity, for God takes us seriously. Christianity, in particular, is a challenge to a choice, and it is a warning that you or I can make the wrong choice.

I *don't* believe that a person who says No to God at the end — if there is to be such a person — will be 'condemned to be tormented endlessly'. That is, I don't believe that the traditional pictures of hell should be taken literally. The idea of 'God the Judge' may be presented by those pictures so as to suggest that God sends people to hell against their will; that I can't believe, for God is love, and what we call the anger or 'wrath' of God is in reality the tough, demanding side of his love, which wants the best for us. Or the idea of 'punishment' may be presented so as to suggest that people who have rejected God suffer pain for ever; but I think that the *only* pain in hell is the pain of the loss of God, the pain of becoming the worst because we have rejected the best in rejecting God. Or the idea of 'everlasting' hell may be presented in such a way as to suggest that hell is endless; but I think that to go to make the final rejection of God, who is the one source of life, would be to die eternally.

I *don't* believe that getting to heaven depends on what creed we hold. That is, I don't believe that God will send us to hell if we are unable to accept some part of a traditional formula in theology. God cannot take so seriously our feeble attempts to use pictures and phrases about him. The belief that gets us to heaven is the attitude which we adopt in our lives. It is the willingness to turn with praise and loyalty towards any part of God or God's work that we can see. Non-Christians and even atheists can have this willingness, when they admire what is true and lovely. That is the attitude which prepares us to say Yes to God at the end.

I *don't* believe that to experience anything of heaven we have to die first. Here and now we turn towards God (or away from him). Here and now we begin to live (or die) eternally. Although clearly a great change must come over us if we are to enter the glory of God when we die, the change will not mean that everything that has gone before is destroyed as irrelevant. We can glimpse heaven on earth, and what is more we can help to get ourselves ready for it.

And finally, I *don't* believe that the life which we know in our bodies on earth is all the life there is. For once I believe in God, I can't believe that the power of God's love is inferior to the power of death. I can't believe in a loving God who would throw me away like a fag-end in the gutter if I were to be killed on the road this afternoon. I can't believe that God will forget you when you die. And that leads me into what I do believe.

I believe in the God of Jesus Christ. That is, I regard Jesus as the man who more than any other experienced God, and I accept as true the message which he gave about God, although of course he used the pictures and phrases used by first-century Jews. The essence of the experience and message of Jesus was very simple: it was the Fatherhood of God. Because he knew God as *Abba* — an Aramaic phrase for which our equivalent would be 'Daddy' — Jesus took life after death for granted. Many reports of his teaching show this. God will go on being the God of Abraham, Isaac, and Jacob after their deaths. He would still be, and be towards them, 'the God of the living'. God will admit even a penitent thief to Paradise. We might say: God will go on being the God of Tom, Dick, and Harry — if they want. This faith in God was so simple and so sure that people around Jesus were astonished. He claimed to *know*, while the people around him only trusted or hoped. The supreme test came when Jesus himself died — in a very public and humiliating way. Had the reality of death obliterated his claims? No, some of the followers of Jesus had a fresh experience, an experience of his life continuing through death. It was like the kind of experience reported to us by the Spiritualists, only it was very special, for the men who had this experience were the first leaders of the Christian Church. They went into the world with the message that God's reality was stronger than death's; with the message that Jesus was right. I am happy to be a member of the Christian Church, which had this beginning. And I believe in the God who is shown by Jesus and the Church.

Therefore I believe in the God who cares. Jesus said that God cares for birds — and how much more for people! Jesus said that God remembers what people have thought or said — and how much more what people *are*. This is the God in whose care I place my life, as Jesus did on his cross (using a phrase from a psalm which all Jewish children were taught to say on going to bed). I do not know exactly how God will respond to that trust. But now that I know what matters most about the character of God, I find it helpful and encouraging to think that I shall be remembered by God. Of course God's memory of us will be more powerful and altogether better than our own memories of people and things, but the way in which we have happy memories can be a clue, I find, to understanding the way in which God will keep us in eternal life. Certainly one great advantage of thinking about God's memory of us is that it helps me to see that our eternal life is more than this life going on forever; it is a share in God's life and God's glory, when nothing is between God and us. Does that involve what is commonly called 'personal survival'? Well, not if that phrase suggests that no big difference is made by death — that someone killed on his bicycle just goes pedalling along for ever. But you will, I believe, 'survive' in one sense. God will continue to love *you* the *you* he knows, and *you* will have your own place in the glory of the God who is the end of your road. I am sorry that I cannot be clearer, but St. Paul himself, struggling to speak about what changes and what stays the same in eternal glory, had to fall back on talking about a spiritual body!

I believe in the God who is coming and conquering. The message of Jesus was that the reign of God was arriving. Everything and everyone would be placed under God's power — the power of almighty, perfect, infinite, and eternal love. The strange victory of Jesus gave this message a new point and a new power. The Church teaches me the message. I learn from Jesus and the Church that doing God's will on the earth matters greatly. But I learn, too, that there is a life beyond the end of life on the earth. I remember from Handel's *Messiah* the promise: 'He shall reign for ever.' In this faith I live, and I expect that nothing more important will ever be said to you until the day when you die.

DAVID L. EDWARDS

[1] *The Last Things Now* (S.C.M. Press, 1969). That book is mainly a discussion about the Bible, but it refers to other literature.

What does the Church mean by being born again?

I want to remind you first of what happened to me, to you and to all of us when we were born. For some of us this happened a very long time ago indeed: for others not so long. But for all of us the event of birth has been so far the most important event in our life. Its only rival in importance is something that has not yet happened to us — our death. I hope that you don't think that I'm being indelicate in reminding you of what happened at your birth. For how can we possibly know what it means to be born again unless we know what it meant to us to be born at all? The very reason that we don't like thinking about our birth shows that we feel strongly about it. Indeed the evidence goes to show that many of us have buried deep in our unconscious minds the events of our birth; and if under the influence of some drug we do recollect them, they are nearly always painful. I should like to draw your attention to four points in connection with our birth, and in each case I would like to invite you to consider their relevance to spiritual rebirth.

In the first place our birth must have been a trying experience to us. What is more, we did nothing ourselves to assist our birth. It was not our own effort, but the force of our mother's muscles, that impelled us into the world. We had to be pushed through a narrow passage into the light of day. We were under pressure in a tight place. Many doctors have claimed that this experience was so vivid that it persists in our feelings later in life, although of course we do not recognize it as such. The very word *anxiety* comes from a Latin word designating a narrow passage.

When we come to consider rebirth, spiritual rebirth, we should surely look for the same kind of thing. And this is what Jesus himself seems to speak about. 'Enter in by the narrow gate,' he says, 'for narrow is the gate, and straitened is the way that leads into life, and few there be that find it.' Or take the occasion of Jesus's baptism, which must have been for him a kind of spiritual rebirth. We are told in St. Mark that the Spirit forced him into the wilderness, almost as it were in spite of himself. And if this

was true for Jesus, how true must it be for us if we are to be
spiritually reborn! 'The wind blows where it likes; and no one
knows where it comes from or where it is going to: so is everyone
who is born of the Spirit.' People so often feel that they are only
making progress in the spiritual life when everything seems to be
going swimmingly. If they feel emptiness or meaninglessness or
depression or panic, they usually feel that something must be
wrong. It seldom occurs to them that, on the contrary, this may
well mean that things are going right. Of course, some people take
a long time to be born; and in the same way some people take a
long time to be spiritually reborn. For them the pain and the
pressure and the meaninglessness seem to go on and on and on.
For others it seems only a brief period. Individuals may differ,
but the principle remains true for us all. Spiritual pressure
prepares us for spiritual life — or if you like to put it in the more
conventional language of the preacher, the sacrifice of the Cross is
the prelude to the release of the Resurrection.

The second point about our birth is that it was the end of a
comfortable and sheltered existence. Before we were born we
lived effortlessly, cushioned and protected and fed by our
mother. Indeed we were still part of our mother, so that we did
not have to take upon ourselves the strains and stresses of an
individual life. But after we were born, how different it was! A
baby at birth is exposed for the first time to cold and heat, to
pressure and roughness, to nice and nasty sensations. A baby at
birth no longer has oxygen supplied free. He has to breathe in the
cold air, and his very first breath shocks him into a cry. I suppose
the best commentary on our birth is that the first noise we
uttered was a cry. A new-born baby experiences the discomfort
of cold, the effort of breathing, the feelings of hunger; and yet all
this is essential if a baby is to make progress and fulfil the
potentialities within him and grow up into a man. Without these
bewildering and unfamiliar surroundings this would be
impossible.

How often we long to get back to that haven of peace and
security that we had before we were born. How often we feel:
'What bliss it would be to have no responsibilities at all! How
marvellous if we could just have peace and security all over again!
How wonderful if we could just sink ourselves in someone else's
personality and forget everything else!' When we feel like
that — and we all do from time to time, especially if we are
frightened or bewildered — then we are probably unconsciously
harking back to the security we had before we were born. I fear

that this has played a large part in the popular conception of heaven. Heaven is so often portrayed as a haven, a kind of return to the womb rather than as the state in which mature persons can together worship God and enjoy him for ever.

Now if birth means the loss of peace and security, so also must spiritual rebirth. We can no longer lean on the convictions of others. We can no longer take things for granted on the authority of others. Jesus told his disciples: 'Launch out into the deep.' Spiritual rebirth means that we have to live the life of a mature individual person: we can no longer be cushioned and protected and insulated against the heat and the cold of life. Often one hears people say: 'If only we could rely on the authority of Mother Church and place ourselves unreservedly under her protection.' Let us be quite clear that such people are very far indeed from spiritual rebirth. Indeed, they are going in the opposite direction! They remind us of Nicodemus's question: 'Can a man go back a second time into his mother's womb?' For that is just what these people would like to do: they want to escape from the responsibilities of personal existence and return to that unreflective peace and security which they had in the womb.

Spiritual rebirth means the very opposite. It means maturity. It means subjecting ourselves to the buffetings of life, and responding to its stimuli. It means no longer an effortless existence, but reliance on our own convictions and on our own experience of life, our own relationship with God. Of course we do not stand alone. We belong as Christians within the Christian society; but our relations with others, if we are spiritually reborn, must be characterized by maturity and not by dependence.

There is a third characteristic of the new-born. At birth we experienced first: we understood much later. We had a whole set of impressions and sensations that were quite new. When we were new-born babes we could not identify those sensations, still less were we able to think about them. We certainly could not place them within any coherent pattern. All we could do was to experience them; the feel of the hands that gripped us and bathed us, the sensation of being lifted up and put down, the feel of the clothes and blankets in which we were tucked up, the pangs of hunger, the sounds of talk and the noise of doors opening and shutting. Only much later did some kind of pattern emerge so that these sensations began to fall into place; and only much later still, as the baby begins to turn into a boy or a girl, could there be any understanding of the cause and the meaning of these sensations.

Isn't this the same with most of our life? Don't we experience first, and only later begin to understand? And isn't this true also of spiritual rebirth? First the experience, and only later, and very gradually, the meaning and the understanding of the experience. Like the experience of birth, rebirth too will have its bitter as well as its pleasant sensations; and all of them will be strange and all of them will be bewildering. But we cannot wait until we can understand Christianity before we can be reborn. If that were so, we would have to wait for ever. No, first we experience God, and only gradually do we begin to be self-conscious about what is happening, and to understand what God has done and is doing to us.

Finally, there is a fourth characteristic. In the womb we existed without any effort at all on our part. We did not even have to put out any effort or energy to be born — it was all done for us. But once we were in the world it was utterly different. We still had to be looked after, of course, because we were only very small and defenceless and helpless little bundles. But still, unless we ourselves had made an effort, we should not have survived. We had to breathe — no one gave us oxygen any more. We had to work to get our satisfactions. We had to use our mouths to suck, and our hands to grip. If we needed help, we had to cry, or no one would have known that we were in trouble. The day we were born was the day when we had to start to make an effort.

Isn't it the same again with spiritual rebirth? We still need to be fed, because, in the words of the First Epistle of Peter, we are 'new-born babes, longing for the spiritual milk which is without guile, that we may grow thereby to salvation, if we have tasted that the Lord is gracious.' Yes, we need food for the spiritual life; but it is equally true that we would perish in the spiritual life unless we made a real effort; an effort to live up to the teaching of our Lord, an effort to grow in our understanding of the Christian faith, an effort to lay hold on the world and to transform it for Christ.

Let me try briefly to sum up what I have said. Birth and rebirth both mean passing through a narrow place, through pain and discomfort, into light and air. Birth and rebirth both mean leaving the security and the peace that responsibility inevitably shatters. Birth and rebirth both mean experiencing new and bewildering sensations long before we can really understand them. Birth and rebirth both mean that, for the survival of life, it is necessary to put out effort and to make a mark in the world.

These are the normal accompaniments of birth. I am not talking about exceptions but the norm; and I hope that I have said enough to convince you that spiritual rebirth is much more than a metaphorical way of saying that a fresh start is being made. Don't imagine for a moment that a few drops of water, sprinkled on your head at your christening, could possibly bring about all this. All it could do was to initiate and to symbolize rebirth. And please don't think that spiritual rebirth is an easy thing, a quick or a slick emotional experience. It cannot be brought about by the mere appeal of a preacher or by a quick decision by the hearer. It is something that penetrates to the very roots of our personality; and it does not come out of the blue. Just as a birth does not take place without nine months of intensive preparation, so spiritual rebirth can only take place when we are ready for it and our time has come. It is as dangerous to try to force it as it is to induce a premature birth.

All that we can do — and it is a great deal — is to open ourselves to God through Christ in faith, hope and love so that he can start to make those intensive preparations that will precede it. But remember that we dare not evade it. 'Unless a man be born again he cannot see God.'

HUGH MONTEFIORE

Is there any truth in Spiritualism, and what is the Church's attitude to it?

Belief in ghosts and uncanny happenings goes back about as far as human history itself. 'Ghost' is of course completely synonymous with 'spirit'. We read of such apparitions in the folklore of bygone days. Primitive peoples in our own day are also generally inclined to credulity in such affairs. Their beliefs, as recorded, have been plausibly explained by modern psychologists and anthropologists by reference to dreams and the other well-known data of psychological and psychoanalytical inquiry.

A typical belief of such peoples is that certain physical objects are invested with *mana*, a dynamic force they talk about as if it behaved somewhat like electricity or radioactivity, being able to wreak terrible destruction when not harnessed by a magician or the like for purposes beneficial to the tribe. This particular primitive belief is called by anthropologists 'dynamism' from the Greek word *dynamis*, meaning 'power'. There are *echoes* of this ancient primitive belief in the New Testament, where we are told (Mark 5:30) that a woman, by touching our Lord's clothes, drew some 'power' (*dynamis*) out of him. At a similar stage people view the world around them as full of 'spirits'. To this belief is given the name 'animism' from the Latin word *anima*, meaning literally 'breath' or 'breeze', for in primitive thought the spirit and life of a man are identified with his breath. Belief in the agency of such 'spirits' persists, often half jokingly, long after people, having become literate and reflective, develop highly critical capacities. Again, there are echoes of such a belief in what we do on Hallowe'en, which is the popular name of the Vigil of (evening before) All Saints' Day or the Feast of All Hallows. Hallowe'en is a sort of 'ghost night' partially christianized. I say 'partially' because though we laugh about 'ghosts' we may still be secretly just a little frightened of them, even without being fully aware of our own fear. Primitive peoples are very frightened of them indeed; but Christian teaching is that since our Lord has power over all things that might hurt us, we have nothing to fear so long as he is with us.

We find that a great poet like Homer took the land of ghosts very seriously: he depicts it, however, as a rather dreary underground world, a limbo of diminished reality to which the dead go, becoming pale shadows of their former selves and moving about soundlessly and colourlessly as we see people doing in our dreams. Homer was probably expressing a typical viewpoint of his day when he writes that he would rather be a poor man in the land of the living than a king in the land of shades. Yet no less typically did the ancients believe that ghosts are 'real'; that is, they took ghosts to be not mere figments of our fancy but independent agencies of some sort, capable of appearing to and even conversing with human beings and also of causing them harm or bringing them good. On the whole, they expected ghosts to be trouble-makers. Ghosts tend to come back to haunt their own old surroundings, and since they have no rightful place in our world, they should be discouraged from doing so, unless perhaps for the purpose of our getting important information from them that would otherwise be inaccessible. Old folk tales are full of such notions.

Modern spiritism,[1] though historically not disconnected with such primitive beliefs, is a much more mature and cultivated development. More importantly, the phenomena with which spiritism today is concerned (which include telepathy and hypnotism as well as table-rapping and the like) have been considered by modern scholars and scientists to be worthy of close scrutiny. Scientific interest in such phenomena may be said to date from about the middle of the last century when certain weird occurrences reported in the United States attracted widespread attention, and led to the founding of societies of interested scientists and other learned inquirers in London, Cambridge, Paris and other centres in Europe as well as in America. An enormous mass of reports, critical studies and analyses has been accumulated by various groups of scientific investigators, not least in the *Proceedings* of the Society for Psychical Research, a British society founded in 1882 by F. W. H. Myers and Edmund Gurney under the presidency of Henry Sidgwick. Myer's *Human Personality and Its Survival of Bodily Death*, which treated the whole subject of psychic phenomena up to the year 1900, is an early classic in the field, forming part of its vast literature in many languages. Extensive, serious scientific work continues to be done in psychical research. There is, for instance, an important American centre for this sort of study at Duke University. During the last hundred years, many very eminent scholars and scientists have interested themselves in the subject. Among especially popular writers who in their day have studied and have been deeply impressed by the evidence may be reckoned men as diverse as Aldous Huxley and that pioneer of detective fiction, Sir Arthur Conan Doyle, the creator of Sherlock Holmes.

The scope such a field offers to impostors and charlatans is obvious, especially in the enterprise of seeking communication with the departed. Some of the unscrupulous mediums who practise spiritism for gain are as patently phony as a six-pound note. Others, sheltering behind a religious façade and exploiting the emotional distress and anguish of bereaved persons who are often an easy prey to their hoaxes, are difficult to expose for the cruel adventurers they are. From the fraud of rogues, however, nothing can be deduced about the phenomena themselves, and a basic purpose of investigations in the area of psychical research is to discover whether, apart from the known perpetration of frauds, there are in fact aspects of or elements in the phenomena that cannot be explained in terms of the accepted findings and ordinary procedures of physics, chemistry and other modern sciences.

The evidence points strongly, and I think in some cases incontestably, to the presence of such aspects or elements that cannot be accounted for in terms of 'ordinary', naturalistic hypotheses. For instance, there are innumerable cases (far too many to explain away as coincidences) such as that of a mother who, in England, suddenly feels a presentiment of her son's death in, say, Australia or Japan, publicly maintains it against scoffing sceptics, and then learns soon after by cable or radio that he had been killed at the very moment when her foreboding came to her with its compelling sense of certitude. Hypnosis is a phenomenon that is familiar to almost everybody. I have seen a skilful hypnotist put on a very amusing as well as thought-provoking show. Hypnotism is also used as a technique for producing the same effect as chemically induced anaesthesia for a surgical operation. So there are *some* psychic phenomena that are not to be explained away. Finally, even in the highly suspect realm of motor automatism, table rapping and the like, the evidence points to the presence of a factor that seems to be beyond the scope of 'ordinary scientific explanation'.

When we go on to ask, however, to what *precisely* the evidence does point, the answer cannot be nearly so definite or so assured. It is one thing to establish negatively as certainly as anything can be so established that a certain phenomenon is not susceptible to any known 'ordinary scientific explanation'; it is another and very different thing to show what the 'real' explanation is. Even a physical phenomenon as commonplace as static electricity could, if we knew nothing at all about it, make plausible the hypothesis that a being from another planet, or a being in a dimension of existence unknown to us, was entering into the situation. We might well even seriously entertain the notion that such a being was trying to communicate an intelligible message to us.

So much for an obvious sceptical protest. On the other side we must now note that modern psychoanalysis gives us a general understanding of the nature of the human soul (*psyche*), in its conscious and subconscious aspects, that is extremely convincing. Very narrow positivistic scientists may and do disallow the methodologies that the rest of us think Freud and Jung have used with great success; but there is no reason to allow ourselves to be trapped into the particular manacles into which positivists want to put our wrists, so long as we find, as most of us do, that the general conclusions of modern psychoanalysis do help us to interpret the working of our own minds in accord with our own experience. Nevertheless, what the psychoanalysts tell us cuts in two ways. On the one hand it greatly helps to show us the kind of forces that are at work 'in the depth of our souls'. This understanding of ourselves brings to light factors at work in us that before were hidden from us, mysteriously wrapped in obscurity. On the other hand, however, what they tell us also provides an often equally plausible explanation of the alleged communications from a 'spirit world', namely, that we and others associated with the quest for access to communications from that hypothetical world are obliquely providing the materials out of which the spiritistic medium *constructs* the communications. By this I do not mean, of course, that he is necessarily engaging in any fraudulent transaction. On the contrary, he might well be at least as much the victim of the psychological forces that are involved as are the other participants.

One of the features of spiritistic communications that seems to me singularly striking is their triviality. There is no reason, I suppose, to expect to hear scintillating wit from 'the other side' just because it is given out to be a 'spirit world', free of the encumbrances of our earthly plane or dimension of existence. Still, one may surely be justified in expecting, by the law of averages, something more interesting than the banalities that we

commonly hear. If our loved ones happen to be a little
pedestrian, perhaps we should not expect them to change
radically into brilliant wits just by crossing the death-barrier; but
the standard of communication is usually unenlivened by even
the sort of exciting news one would expect from a friend who has
been to Paris or Pisa for a week's holiday. One cannot but
wonder, then, how anybody could really go into another
dimension of existence and then surmount the barrier of death,
to come back merely to engage in talk so dull that it makes even
our own conversation sound almost as lively as that of the
dialogue in a clever play. To say the least, all this tends to dispose
us to suspect that the hypothetical 'spirit communications', being
less vivacious and informative than the people attending the
séance could have produced by themselves, does in fact come
from themselves rather than from those from whom, by any
reckoning, one would expect interesting talk. Honestly, if I were
in such a 'spirit world', I can't see myself going to the trouble to
come back here unless I had something more to say than is
usually said through mediums.

When all that is said, however, we must admit that one does
occasionally hear of a very remarkable occurrence or startling sort
of communication that does oblige us to remain very open to the
possibility that real communication is 'coming through'. Even so,
from whence is it coming? From what kind of a world is it?
Generally, we are asked to believe that it is a world inhabited by
our departed friends who are engaged there in another sort of life
beyond this one and who find time, or take time out of their
work there, to try to get messages across to us. There is certainly
no scientific evidence to make such a view untenable; but we
should ask: even if tenable, is it in the least likely or plausible, *if*
other explanations seem to meet the case?

There is also another and very fearsome possibility that should
not be excluded from our openminded inspection of the
possibilities. The communications might be indeed from some
other dimension of existence – a world hostile to us, eager to
mislead and deceive us, and in the last resort bent upon our
destruction. My own mother, who happened to find, while still a
young woman, that she seemed to have very strong capabilities
that contemporary spiritists acclaimed as psychical, was led, after
some experimentation, to such a conclusion. In reaching it she
was much influenced by a curious happening. At a spiritistic
séance there had been a great deal of activity: messages were
coming through copiously and furniture seemed to be jumping

about all over the place. Then a member of the party, a devout
Christian inquirer, uttered the words: 'Do you know that God
became man for us and for our salvation?' At this, everything
instantly stopped. There was not a single rap or message, and
after a while everybody went home. The same thing occurred on
a subsequent occasion, with exactly the same results. My mother,
for the rest of her life, was very antagonistic to the whole
spiritistic undertaking, which she accounted highly dangerous,
taking the view that while our Lord guards his faithful people
against every sinister force that would radically hurt us, we have
no business to be dabbling in spiritistic adventures in places where
Jesus Christ is not lovingly and explicitly acknowledged as Lord
of all. Her comparatively brief period of experimentation not
only reinforced her in the Scottish Kirk's orthodoxy in which she
had been nurtured; it also convinced her that attempts had been
made by hostile psychic forces to deprive her of the Christian
heritage she ever after prized even more highly than before. I
offer no comment on her conviction, except that it is not unique
and that it does exhibit, at any rate, another possibility that
neither practitioners of spiritism nor those who pooh-pooh it
commonly entertain at all.

What if the answer to the first part of the question before us
were that there is indeed truth in spiritism, and what if the truth
be that the medium's table is a 'table of devils' (1 Cor. 10:21), a
sinister realm of existence in another dimension that we should
be much better off without? Of course I am not *giving* that
answer. I am only saying that the possibility cannot be excluded.

As an Anglican priest, I am reminded every time I celebrate
the Holy Eucharist that I do so in the presence of more people
than are physically observable. There may be only twenty of us
visible at the altar; but The Other, the Risen Christ is there with
us. Moreover, we are joined to the whole company of God's
people throughout the world and throughout all history, the
whole Church on both sides of the Death Curtain. This is what
the Celebration has always meant, and without that part of its
meaning it would mean nothing at all. As I say the astoundingly
beautiful and awesome words, 'Therefore with angels and
archangels, and with all the company of heaven, we laud and
magnify thy glorious Name, evermore praising thee . . .', I know
we are not alone. We are, in the antique, traditional language of
the English Bible, 'compassed about with so great a cloud of
witnesses' (Heb. 12:1), in such a way that the twenty or two
hundred of us that I could count by pointing are only a fraction

of that multitude who are gathered with us around the Table of our Lord. Alongside every communicant who kneels at the altar are his most beloved friends, feeding there with him at their common eucharistic Feast.

In some modern versions of our Christian liturgy, after the priest has made solemn remembrance of ancient heroes of the Church like Paul and Clement and Cyprian, individuals will voice the names of others who are much in their hearts, such as Grandad or Aunt Bessie or even the dear old man at the grocer's whose name we never knew but who always had a smile for everybody even when he knew he was dying of cancer. Only those unimaginatively blind to what is going on in the interstices at church can, in Francis Thompson's phrase, 'miss the many-splendoured thing', and so fail to see

the traffic of Jacob's ladder
Pitched betwixt Heaven and Charing Cross.

Now we must surely ask ourselves a crucial question. If my deceased friends wished to communicate with me, at what address would they be likely to call? What would be the most convenient and proper trysting place to meet a Christian? Why, of course, in the central act of Christian worship, where we are looking out for the whole company of earth and heaven, and where we are therefore on the *qui-vive* for the spirits of all the creatures of our God. As surely as I would look for a studious boy in the library or an athletic one in the gymnasium, they would look for a Christian at God's altar, around which we habitually foregather in awareness and expectation of the living God we know in Christ our Saviour. Here is the only adequately engineered bridge across the abyss of death, the only true gateway to all spirits of our God. Every time we celebrate the Eucharist, we, finding ourselves, in the words of the Lesson for the Epistle on All Saints' Day, in company with 'a great multitude, which no man could number, of all nations, and kindreds, and peoples, and tongues' (Rev. 7:9), are more open than at any other time to whatever influence our departed loved ones may wish to exert upon us.

Here, moreover, is the only place I would care to meet them, for if a spirit were planning to meet me elsewhere I would not readily trust him. I would be asking myself: 'Why doesn't he want to see me at our own House, the House of God, in the midst of the Family, where the Feast is spread? That is where I always meet my friends, and all my friends know it.' Why, even my non-Christian friends (I have several very good ones who have died) would look for me there if they looked anywhere.

Where else? It is almost daylight in the little church, and the altar candles, symbol of the light our Lord brings into the world, are now aflame. Deep expectant silence pervades the whole building where the Communion is about to begin. You can feel the traffic 'between Heaven and Charing Cross' already beginning, though it has not reached its peak. You can't hear exactly what that old negro is praying behind the gnarled hands with which he is covering his lips, or what the prim little lady is asking beneath her mask-like face; nor can you see much behind the goggly eyes of the boy who seems to be just staring into nothingness. Yet you must be practically dead yourself if you can't feel the agonies and the joys that are rising from them all. People are still gathering. A few stragglers are coming in, and as they do you feel the number of worshippers is somehow increasing not in an arithmetical but in a geometrical progression.

As the drama of the Holy Communion unfolds, the traffic intensifies. The priest, solemnly making the sign of our salvation and using the ancient and eloquently restrained language of the Prayer Book, utters the Commemoration: 'And we also bless thy holy Name for all thy servants departed this life in thy faith and fear.' Surely nobody can be so stone deaf as not to hear the unuttered lone cry in the mysterious silence on the other side of the altar rails: 'Oh, Peggy, how I have missed you!' and the unspoken 'Dear Bob, how can I live without you?' If then, a few minutes later, you were a priest administering the Host and Chalice and could not in your mind's eye see beside the communicants their loved ones attending them and sharing with them in a common ecstasy, a common delight in the radiance of the Presence of our Risen Lord, your Imagination Quotient would have to be zero.

And if, outside the church door afterwards some spiritists were to invite me to a *séance*, I would tell them I needed it about as much as the Bank of England needs a bent penny with a hole in it. I believe that answer accords with the Mind of the Church.

> Those who love thee break all barriers;
>   With them let me run:
> Only in thy household can I
>   Share the family fun.

GEDDES MACGREGOR

[1] The word 'spiritualism' has been traditionally used, as are its counterparts in other languages (e.g., French *spiritualisme* and Spanish *espiritualismo*), in an important special sense that has nothing to do with a belief that departed spirits communicate with and show themselves to human beings, which is the sense plainly intended in the question before us. In French there is no ambiguity: *spiritisme* is always used for the secondary, popular sense that is intended here and is the dictionary translation of the English word 'spiritualism' as used in this sense. Following the practice of some other writers, who prefer risking pedantry to courting ambiguity, I use, in my attempt to answer the question posed, the term 'spiritism'.

What does the Church mean by the Devil?

I remember during the war coming back for a night to my college, and finding myself in Hall next to Bertrand Russell. Seeing I had on a clerical collar, Russell kindly began the conversation with a topic a clergyman could be expected to understand and be interested in. 'Tell me' he said – 'Tell me, are Christians still obliged to believe in the Devil?' I was young, and the answer I gave was so impudent that it makes me blush to think of it – 'Christians', I said, 'would regard your disbelief in the Devil as one of his greatest triumphs.'

But ever since then my mind has been intermittently plagued by the subject. It came back to me for instance, that when I was a child an aunt of mine, presumably considering the atmosphere of my home rather too religious, said to me when we were alone together, 'Don't forget, Harry, that it would be a dull world, if there were no Devil.' And I suppose in a way she converted me, though it was not a sudden conversion.

The first thing that occurs to me is that the Devil is terribly mixed up. That, I know, is what one generally says nowadays about the people one dislikes. But I don't mean it quite in that sense. I mean that the Devil is a symbol for a mixed bag of contradictory tendencies. His picture is used to typify forces and feelings which are not consistent with each other. He is a myth which speaks at the same time of intense excitement and intolerable boredom. He is both a whizz-kid and a deadly old fiend. He appears to offer both a thrilling life in a James Bond paradise and a living death in a derelict deserted shanty-town. He combines fun and futility –

> When Boris used to call in his Sedanca,
> When Teddy took me down to his estate,
> When my nose excited passion,
> When my clothes were in the fashion,
> When my beaux were never cross if I was late;

There was sun enough for lazing on the beaches,
There was fun enough for far into the night,
But I'm dying now and done for,
What on earth was all the fun for?
For I'm old and ill and terrified and tight.[1]

Well, that expresses the traditional view of the ambiguity surrounding the Devil. The Devil offers you life, thrills, satisfaction − in the present. But these are only bait by means of which you get hooked for the future, and it is a very long future, in which you subsist in a tormented state, even if, like Goethe's Faust, you eventually emerge. The point is the ambiguity, traditionally expressed in terms of time present and time future. Fun now. Futility later.

I don't think our age can express the ambiguity in those terms, for two main reasons. First, we are aware now in the present of both the fun and the futility. In varying degrees each is real to us and each contemporary. Secondly, to us it seems somehow immoral to use the present as a sort of insurance policy for the future. We must judge the value of what we do in terms of itself and not in terms of careful calculations about what it may do to us in some remote possible future. For that would be to kill all spontaneity, a crime against life. So we must approach the Devil's ambiguity by another road.

But here I must be dull, and explain more precisely what I mean by the Devil. Lady Bracknell was described by her nephew as unfair because she was a monster without being a myth. The Devil is unfair because he is a myth without being a monster. He isn't a person with horns and a tail. Nor is he a sort of ethereal equivalent of that. He isn't what we'd call personal at all. But he is none the less a myth, by which in this case I mean not something unreal which isn't there, but something too real and too powerfully present to be described directly or literally, something therefore which we have to describe indirectly by means of pictures. The Devil can be thought and spoken of only mythologically. The old mythological picture of a personal spirit walking about the world seeking whom he may devour spoke meaningfully to past ages. It doesn't speak to us, so we have to use other pictures or myths to describe the same reality.

The myths which speak meaningfully to our era are those drawn from the human psyche, from the descriptions of psychic mechanisms elaborated by Freud and his successors. That is the language we now understand. But I want to stress that I am using this language as an attempt to clothe in some sort of mythological form realities which go beyond it. So please don't imagine that I think the Devil is no more than a psychological process. There is in the world, I believe, a reality of evil, a force, if you like, making for evil whose presence we cannot explain, and of whose origins Christians must admit they are totally ignorant. I shall not therefore be concerned to justify the existence of evil in the light of Christian belief in a good and omnipotent God, because, although many have attempted to do it, I don't think it can be done. All I intend to do is to describe how evil impinges upon our individual and quite ordinary lives, and to examine the ambiguity of what it offers. To do this I shall use the mythology of psychological analysis, hoping that the myth will not be mistaken for a photograph.

The human psyche seeks equilibrium. It wants to establish within itself an even balance of forces. That is what we mean by stability in a person. A stable person is not pulled about from one extreme to another extreme. He is not, shall we say, passionately ingratiating at one moment and outrageously rude at another. You don't find him not opening his mouth one week and never pausing for breath the next. By and large he is always the same and you can rely on his reactions to circumstances. You can forecast fairly accurately whether he will be pleased, hurt, angry, or amused. Nobody I suppose, possesses a perfect equilibrium of this kind. But most people approximate to it in some degree or other, and there is in everybody a built-in urge towards it. Stability is something we all want to attain. Every human being is searching for it. To be knocked off our balance, as we say, is not considered by us to be a normal state of affairs. We feel that the disturbance of our equilibrium needs explaining while its maintenance does not. In this psychic realm equilibrium is very largely equated with goodness. Popular phrases are often revealing. The American phrase — 'to feel good' is a case in point. When it is said that a man feels good or that it's our duty to make other people feel good, what is being described is the maintenance or restoration of psychic equilibrium. Hence, too, I imagine, the attractive pull of ideologies, political or religious. What an ideology offers its devotees, whether it be the Communist party or the Conservative Evangelicals, is precisely that equilibrium which we intuitively recognize as a primary good. And we can have it even when, or perhaps especially when, we are caught up in a crusading war. The dragon is very useful to St. George. It makes him feel good. But the point has been elaborated enough. In the instinctive realm of feeling, in the realm of psychic reality, equilibrium is equated with goodness. And the converse of course follows inevitably. In the same psychic realm, what threatens to disturb equilibrium is equated with evil. To the infant the sense of oneness he gets when sucking his mother's breast is goodness. The sense of disruption he gets when the breast is withdrawn is evil. In the adult world an example of the same sort of feeling-reaction is the howl of condemnation which greets the arrival of some new art-form — in literature, painting, or music. It is infamous. It is evil. It overturns the apple-cart of aesthetic equilibrium. It does not make members of the establishment feel good.

But although for the psyche equilibrium is felt to be a primary good, there is combined with this a potential suspicion that it may be being preserved at too high a price. The psychic police who maintain law and order in the personality are potentially suspected of stifling liberty and inhibiting growth. When these potential suspicions begin to be actualized, then comes the feeling that peace is not so much being preserved as being enforced, and that the enforcement is a very expensive business involving such a high rate of taxation that we are left very much poorer than we need be. Peace, in other words, is being bought at the expense of life. The primary good of equilibrium is felt to shut out too much. And it is precisely at this point that evil begins to look increasingly ambiguous. Evil, remember, was felt to be that which upsets the apple-cart. But now we begin to feel so constricted that we wonder whether this evil, this threat to equilibrium, may not after all be a good. Perhaps instead of shutting it out, we should invite it in. Perhaps the disturber, the destroyer, may have some greater good to offer us. What is being described is a psychic awakening to the possibilities of life, possibilities which, if they are to become realities, must involve feelings of danger.

A terrible dilemma, this psychic awakening presenting us with a confusion of values. What is now our good? What is now our evil? That which we once felt to be our evil is now beginning to look at least a lesser evil than what was once felt to be our good. What has disappeared from the inner world of the psyche is the absolute contrast between good and evil. The equilibrium we once felt to be wholly good, is still good. We can't deny that. But it is no longer felt as unqualified good. The sinister disturbance is still felt to be evil, but again not unqualified. We feel it may also be good, and even a necessary good for us of which the denial would involve a loss of integrity. Should we not be traitors to ourselves if we refused to have any truck whatever with it? For is it not now felt to be good as well as evil? 'And I said, O that I had wings like a dove, for then would I flee away, and be at rest.' But we haven't got wings. We can't flee away.

The most obvious example of this dilemma is sexual desire. Freud surely was right in thinking that lust was a destroyer which fully indulged would make impossible the creation of those masterpieces of art and science which are humanity's glory. But he also saw clearly that a personality organized against the acceptance of sexual desire is equally sterile.

A less noticed example of this dilemma, though equally important, is the instinct of aggression. Those who consider themselves progressive are often curiously blind to the existence of aggression in the human psyche. Sex, they tell us, is here to stay and it is hypocritical nonsense not to admit it. At the same time they often imagine that aggression can be abolished simply by pretending it doesn't exist and holding up placards labelled Peace. But the stern truth is — and it is horribly stern — that in the long run nothing is going to make nuclear war more likely than the fatuous fallacy that man is not an aggressive being. Man's aggressive instincts, like his sexual instincts, destructive though they obviously are from one point of view, and so felt as evil, are not unqualified evil and from another point of view can be felt as good, and so admitted into consciousness in spite of the disturbances there they will undoubtedly cause. For it is by the awareness of his aggressive potential that man finds the dynamic which leads to achievement. It is by aggression that things get done. In our former *laissez-faire* society, human aggression was given the opportunity to actualize itself in the struggle for economic survival or economic domination. I am not in any way advocating a return to *laissez-faire* even if it were possible, which mercifully it is not. But it remains true that the Welfare State has not yet discovered what to do with aggression. Far from facing this issue, the Welfare State seems to be turning its back on it. 'Know ye not' said St. Paul 'that they which run in a race run all, but one receiveth the prize? So run, that ye may obtain.' But in our society we are so bemused by the sacred cow of equality that everybody gets the prize whether he tries to run or not.

I am not at all concerned with issues of fairness or unfairness. What I am trying to point out is the appalling danger involved in the gradual elimination of ways and means by which people may recognize and give expression to their aggressive potential. For a man feels a traitor to himself unless and until he admits this demon to his hearth and home. And only when so admitted will the demon become only half a demon, and the rest a god of power.

There is the original psychic equilibrium. Then comes into my awareness various psychic forces which, because they threaten the equilibrium, are instinctively felt as evil. Yet to deny this evil entry into consciousness, to turn away from it and think of something else, to deny such evils entry on the policy of peace at any price, is felt as a sort of murder of the self, a fundamental disloyalty to one's human nature. For if you invite in the lust and aggression, although it will upset your former equilibrium, it will also bring to you raw material capable of being woven into a richer, more rewarding, life. In time you will establish a new more comprehensive equilibrium, more comprehensive because more of your potential will be creatively released and activated. And it is not only you who will benefit. The community of which you are a member will also be enriched. The world will become a more worthwhile place. You will be making your contribution to the treasury of human value.

But alas, that is not of course the whole story, not by any manner of means. For the ambiguity of evil remains. It is not simply changed once and for all into good. Its potential as evil remains. It can still destroy as well as create. And it is of this continuing ambiguity that the Faust story and other similar legends speak with such frightening eloquence. But I do not intend here to mangle the utterances of genius. I am going to approach this continuing ambiguity of evil by a parable of my own — a parable simple and crude. It is concerned with eating. So far my diet has been restricted to bread and milk. I can exist on that, but I shan't grow very strong and robust. So I take the risk of eating other things beside. I eat a steak. Chewing it up is a bit frightening, but I'm feeling rather brave, so I go ahead and begin to enjoy the meal, to enjoy it very much. There is a good chance of my digesting it satisfactorily. If I do, it will give me the nutrition I need. The steak will become part of my own physical make-up, and will help to make me strong. I know several people who eat steaks regularly and they are very strong. But, of course, in my case, there may well be a less fortunate result. I may not be able to digest the steak properly. And if that happens, for me it will not be nutritious. It will not become part of my physical make-up. On the contrary, it will gurgle about inside me and make me ill. I shall feel horribly bilious and probably be sick. In all, I shall be very much weaker than if I had stuck to my customary bread-and-milk. Of course I know that certain things like rotten fruit or bad fish always make people ill. And I wasn't such a fool as to eat those. But good steaks? What am I to do? Must I continue for ever to eat on the assumption that all that is not bread and milk is poison? The answer is Yes. Yes, if you are not prepared to take risks.

And let there be no mistake about the risk, the appalling risk, of unlocking the citadel of the psyche to let in the forces waiting to enter. Instead of being the Devil's host, you may become his slave. The psychic forces you have admitted into your conscious personality may not bring you the creative release they seemed to promise. For you may not be able to assimilate them, to make them into an integral part of what you are. And then instead of becoming a true and valid expression of your total self, they will kick about with an unrelated life of their own. And thus they will undo you, destroying even the meagre creative potential you once had.

I said earlier on that I believed there was in the world a reality of evil, a force making for evil. I can now explain what I meant. How, with any self-respect, can I confine myself to the diet of bread and milk? Yet, when I summon up the courage to eat meat, and the meat destroys me, is not that evil, diabolical evil in the ultimate sense, evil for which I am in no way responsible? When that which was ordained to life, I find to be unto death?

Yet to very few, almost certainly to none of us here, will the drama turn out to be on this heroic scale of final tragedy. We are not quite the stuff Macbeths are made of. For us there will be a mixture — a mixture of excitement and boredom, of paradise and shanty town, of fun and futility, of elation and depression, now one aspect predominating, now the other. But as we pass through these ups and downs we shall slowly be assimilating the psychic forces we have allowed to enter. The mixture will become less of a mixture and more of an integrated whole. But it won't happen in a day, nor can the pace be forced, and we shall move backwards as well as forwards like the waves of the incoming tide. There is nothing for it, if we want to live. We must face and receive the ambiguity. We have no choice. If we want life, that is.

Of course we can always capitulate and choose not to live, choose to remain permanently on our bread and milk, unaware that we have incurred what has been described as the true guilt. And let there be no mistake, it can lead you to an extremely successful career and a fat income.

'See, I have set before you this day life and good, and death and evil. Therefore choose life.' But have we the courage? Yes, if we have the faith. The faith I mean is spoken of by different people in different ways, and it can be possessed by those who don't know they have it, and it is found in all races in all parts of the world. Many would call it confidence in life, and I wouldn't want to quarrel with that description. But I myself can describe it only as faith that nothing can separate us from the love of God, things present or things to come, things outside us or things within us, what we call evil or even what we call goodness — that nothing in heaven or on earth can separate us from the love which has conquered everything because it has suffered everything.

HARRY WILLIAMS

[1] 'Sun and Fun', *Collected Poems* (1958) by John Betjeman (London, John Murray) p.216.

How can we know God's will?

One of the phrases commonly used in religious circles is 'doing God's will'. But what is 'God's will'? What does he wish me to do? Unless there is some way of finding out what he wills, is it not a meaningless phrase, adding nothing to 'What ought I to do?' 'What is right?'

The witness of the saints is that it is possible to know God's will, and to perform it, if not perfectly, at least in some degree. And yet the claim that this *is* God's will is a very dangerous claim to make, because it suggests that I am certainly right, and that anyone who disagrees with me or thwarts me must be the enemy of God.

God does guide, but not usually by means of a short cut. There are stories about 'guidance', the main point of which is that there was no rational means whatever of knowing what ought to be done. The saintly Bishop Pakenham Walsh used to tell how he found his way to a bungalow in the hills of Assam. It was quite dark, and at each fork in the path he asked, 'Which way, Lord?' and the Lord said 'Go to the right . . .' or to the left, or straight on, as the case might be. Finally, he came to a vertical wall which he could not climb, and he said, 'What now, Lord?' and the Lord said, 'Go to the right', and he went to the right, and turned a corner, and there was a door — the vertical wall was the wall of the house he was trying to find. There are other stories of inexplicable impulses, more significant perhaps, which turn out to lead to someone in serious need.

Yes, some specially gifted souls do seem to have an extra sense, and some have learnt to develop it beyond the point to which their five senses and their consecrated common sense have brought them. But faithful obedience in the common ways comes first.

God guides through the instrument which he has brought into being for the purpose of exploring the frontier where his love meets the world; and that instrument is the Church, with yourself, your conscience, your mind, your sensitive self alive to your environment, as his spearhead for action at the precise point in time and space where you find yourself. You are the growing tip there of the living Body; the point where the tradition of the past is growing into the present and creating the future. And so, in any serious matter the first thing to do is to bring to bear the wisdom of the past and the authoritative teaching of the Church, which will rule out certain courses and indicate the general direction. You don't have to worry over the question, 'Should I commit adultery?' The answer is 'No'. You don't have to worry over the question, 'Ought I to love this neighbour as myself?' the answer is 'Yes'. You can then go on to the fascinating question of how to love this neighbour now effectually; and you often get to the point where the rules don't help you much, and you have to improvise; for it is all, as Aristotle said, in the particulars, in the 'How and the Where and the When and the How much?' Some are creative artists in human relations. Most of us are pretty good bunglers, but if we can put ourselves completely at the disposal of God's love, something good will come. I wish we could see Christian morality less as a keeping of rules and more as a creative adventure, in which the rules have a necessary but limited part to play.

It is nonsense to say that there can be no morality without religion, but there are extra possibilities open to those who have learnt to see the world, their neighbours and themselves in the light of what they know of Christ.

To look first for opportunities of helping, to have a view as wide as God's purpose in the world, to value holiness above comfort, to seek first the kingdom of God and to trust him for the rest — these are gifts which the Holy Spirit gives to those who seek them.

Sometimes there are decisions to be taken which will affect your whole career, sometimes agonizing decisions in which it seems that certainty is unattainable; decisions too where two apparent duties clash, or where apparent duty clashes with inclination, where a reasonable prudence conflicts with apparent unselfishness.

In such cases the first and only golden rule is this: *You must promise to do God's will before you know what it is.* It is no use making conditions in advance, and asking to be shown God's will as long as it is not anything unpleasant, as long as it doesn't mean going abroad, as long as it doesn't mean a loss of income, as long as it doesn't mean working with this man, or living alongside that one . . . .

The second rule is, *Be competent and get your facts straight.* This is easier said than done, and part of the object of your education is to give you a competent and not a muddly inefficient mind, at least in some part of the field in which you have to take responsible decisions.

On many matters the wise thing to do will be to seek advice from people who are wiser than yourself.

The third rule is, *Distinguish your own point of responsibility, and decide on that.* You don't have to decide whether to take this job, but whether to apply for it, or, it may be, whether you are to accept it when it is offered. You don't have to decide whether to marry this girl, but whether to propose to her . . . and so on. People sometimes work themselves into a dither trying to decide what the Headmaster ought to do, or the Bishops . . . .

The fourth rule is, *One step enough for me.* Don't cross bridges till you come to them. Don't worry about the thing after next; it may never happen. Of course, you may have to consider more or less distant results in deciding on your present action — you have to find out where the train is going before you get on board. But you can't see very far, and most of the future is quite out of your control, though fortunately not out of God's. So, I would say, Don't be too careful of your future, and be ready to take risks with your career.

And the last rule is this: *Decide, and don't look back.* Don't waste time wishing you hadn't done what you did. It's no use saying 'If only I had decided otherwise.' (You may recognize a mistake so as not to do it again, but that is another thing.) You may decide in uncertainty and still be right. You may feel quite certain and still be wrong. But if you decide in good faith, God will take you on from there, and if you make a mistake, God can use that too.

Such decisions are important, but not so important as they seem at the time. What is important is the good faith of your decision, and how you implement it afterwards. It is easy to offer to be a missionary, hard to be a Christian in the mission field minute by minute and hour by hour for years and years and years. It is one thing, and a very important one, for two people to decide in love to marry one another; it is another, and a greater thing, to remain married, and to practise mutual charity and forgiveness and to build up a Christian home to the glory of God.

'O God, who didst teach the hearts of thy faithful people by the sending to them the light of thy Holy Spirit, grant us by the same Spirit to have a right judgement in all things, and evermore to rejoice in his holy comfort.' That is just what he does for those who ask him, and who mean what they say.

T. R. MILFORD

If one doesn't believe in life after death, and has one's own moral code, what more has Christianity to offer?

Suppose we allowed ourselves sufficient historical licence to imagine that Moses was immediately succeeded by Jesus Christ. To think anachronistically in this way is to remind ourselves that the question we are considering might well have been asked by the early Israelites. For they certainly had no explicit belief in a future life, and they also had one of the best-known of all moral codes. It is true, and from the point of view of this question very significant, that for the Israelites moral and religious prescriptions were inexplicably mixed. But what have been traditionally called the Ten Commandments are certainly in part a moral code. For instance[1]:

'You have six days to labour and do all your work'. But on the seventh day 'you shall not do any work, you, your son or your daughter, your slave or your slave girl, your cattle or the alien within your gates.'

'Honour your father and your mother . . .'.

'You shall not commit murder.'

'You shall not commit adultery.'

'You shall not steal.'

'You shall not give false evidence against your neighbour.'

'You shall not covet your neighbour's house; you shall not covet your neighbour's wife, his slave, his slave girl, his ox, his ass, or anything that belongs to him.'

Let us then look at this idea of a moral code of which the Ten Commandments is one of the best examples. A moral code is a set of rules for social and personal behaviour. But the first point to notice about a moral code is that the mere existence of a moral code does not ensure that the rules which it contains are kept, that the behaviour it prescribes is followed. Rules can be recognized, and perfectly well understood, and yet have no compelling power to ensure that they are kept.

St. Paul in the Epistle to the Romans has much to say about the moral and psychological inadequacies of a set of rules, and though he was admittedly thinking of the vast system of rules called the Jewish Law or Torah, many of the points he makes could be made of any moral code whatever. For instance, says St. Paul[2]: 'Except through law I should never have become acquainted with sin. For example, I should never have known what it was to covet, if the law had not said, "Thou shalt not covet." Through that commandment sin found its opportunity, and produced in me all kinds of wrong desires.' To take a specific example, suppose we are touring in an ancient city and, weary at the end of the day, we are making our way round to the castle when we suddenly see at the end of an unpromising little alley the notice: 'It is forbidden to take this short route to the castle.' What would our reaction be to this prohibition? Would we not say that it was asking to be broken? The gap between the ideals which a moral code often expresses, ideals which in our best moments we acknowledge, and our actual behaviour is frankly and poignantly expressed in one of St. Paul's best known confessions[3]: 'The good which I want to do, I fail to do; but what I do is the wrong which is against my will.' As the Jerusalem Bible translates it: 'Instead of doing the good things I want to do, I carry out the sinful things I do not want.' Paul has said earlier[4]: 'What I do is not what I want to do, but what I detest.' In short, a moral code brings with it, by itself, no guarantee of moral success. On the contrary, a moral code by itself may do no more than make us very conscious of our personal weaknesses and moral failures. A moral code can bring endless frustration which the code by itself cannot remove. A code by itself has no power to overcome the frustration it creates.

By contrast with a moral code, loyalty to a person is in the first place far more compelling especially when that person wins our loyalty by his inspiration and the power, not of some authoritarian dictator, but of love. Even when we fail, even when we are disloyal, in this case we know that there is love to welcome us back. There is now the possibility of frustration being overcome. This is very different indeed from our having to recognize, after failure, that the moral code we had acknowledged as our guide to behaviour is getting further and further from us in terms of practical possibilities.

Further, behaviour which is inspired by a person has far more of that 'inwardness' which is the very essence of true morality than a moral code could ever hope to evoke. If we doubt this, we have only to think of that very detailed moral code which is to be found on ships travelling to the Continent of Europe and to countries abroad, and which specifies the goods whose entry is

prohibited into the United Kingdom. There can be very few
people indeed who, reading these lengthy and detailed notices,
feel strangely moved and inwardly inspired. It is only when a
person is seen to be the very embodiment of a moral code that
the code can have any hope of being inwardly inspiring, of its
rules exercising a reasonable power over us and being kept, and of
our being delivered from the frustration that moral rules by
themselves can generate.

But there is another inadequacy about moral codes as such.
They always need constant revision. Not even the Ten
Commandments remained unchanged. If we turn to the book of
Deuteronomy[5] we shall find some significant changes. For
instance, one of the reasons there given for not working on the
Sabbath day is 'so that your slaves and slave girls may rest as you
do.' Further, in the Tenth Commandment the wife has ceased to
be regarded as a mere chattel, but is given pride of place: 'You
shall not covet your neighbour's wife; you shall not set your heart
on your neighbour's house, his land, his slave, his slave girl, his
ox, his ass, or on anything that belongs to him.'

There was no difficulty in thinking of revisions of the Ten
Commandments because these were set in a religious background
and formed part of a wider loyalty. Expressing one aspect of
God's total claim on men they were always in principle capable of
being revised so as to become a better and more adequate
expression of that claim. Moral obligation was but one way of
acknowledging God's presence, activity, and will. Significantly we
find the Ten Commandments, whether in Exodus or
Deuteronomy, prefaced by the verse: 'I am the Lord your God
who brought you out of Egypt, out of the land of slavery.'
Morality was part of a total response to God. And in the version
of the Commandments in Deuteronomy the Sabbath day's rest is
not related to the creation story, but rather to the knowledge the
Hebrews have of God's activity in history: 'Remember that you
were slaves in Egypt, and the Lord your God brought you out
with a strong hand and an outstretched arm, and for that reason
the Lord your God commanded you to keep the Sabbath day.'

Speaking more generally, it is only when a moral code is
offered as an interpretation, an interim expression, of an eternal
vision that it provides for its own reform and has built-in
possibilities of development. A moral code by itself may express
no more than a soul-destroying conventionalism. Contrariwise, to
see a moral code as an expression of an eternal ideal is, first, to
value it for that very reason, and yet, secondly, because no set of

rules can be an entirely adequate expression of the eternal ideal, we shall always remain dissatisfied and be in principle spurred to moral reform.

So a morality centred on a person does not only give a much greater freedom and spontaneity, a much greater inwardness than one centred on a code; it not only provides us with an antidote to frustration; it can even possess built-in possibilities of revision if that person is in some way or other an expression of eternal ideals, an expression of God in his activity. This is precisely what Christians believe of Christ.

Morality, then, is not best regarded as the keeping of a moral code, but rather as being inspired by an ideal, and best of all such a moral ideal as it embodied is a morally good person. Christianity does not ask for an *imitatio Christi* in the sense of a slavish copying of what Christ said or did. Christian behaviour is rather behaviour which comes from an intimate friendship with Christ, behaviour which comes from living in his presence. We all know how the 'atmosphere' of a school or a club matters far more for the morality of that school or club than any formal rules. So it is with Christian morality. What matters most is our personal relationship with Christ and the 'atmosphere' of those communities which together make up the whole Christian Church.

But there are still difficulties which must be frankly faced. Even when we are tolerably successful in keeping the rules, and saved from the despair to which frustration can lead; and even when we are inspired constantly to revise the rules, our difficulties are not at an end. Even though loyalty to a person, and not least to Christ, is far more successful as the basis of morality than the mere keeping of a moral code, this is not to say that there are no more difficulties. It can often seem as if, despite all our efforts, evil triumphs; that the best plans, carried out with as much sincerity and faithfulness as we can muster, go wrong. In any complex situation, it seems well nigh impossible not to be misunderstood, or to be mistaken, or to be just plainly inadequate. We sometimes speak of this fact as pointing to a 'flaw' in Creation, and though that could never be more than a kind of approximate metaphor, it is a compact way of pointing to an intricate set of facts about human nature and morality.

These are the facts which lie behind the doctrine of Original Sin, though the great pity of that doctrine is that the undoubted facts to which it was meant to point have often been concealed by the metaphysical intricacies, and the dubious inferences, of the discourse in which it has often been expressed. The facts can hardly be questioned, and we need only take a single example. There can be no doubt whatever that in the face of mass unemployment, social insecurity, lack of provision for sickness or retirement, a massive welfare scheme was wanted. Without doubt the authors of such a morally excellent scheme supposed that once these provisions were made security, contentment and peace would replace insecurity, anxiety and despair. But by now, and with hindsight, it is quite clear that something more is wanted if moral aspirations are to come to a satisfactory fruition. It is this final fruition that Christianity would claim to offer. In more traditional terms, it would have its own answer to Original Sin.

Christianity would remind us, in general terms, that moral codes, and social planning in accordance with them, must always reckon with the imperfections of humanity. We must always see that our lives in time are never, even at best, more than a projection in space and time of what truly belongs to eternity and they will always have their tangled threads and disheartening imperfections. But the more particular contribution which Christianity has to offer to this nest of problems is the assurance, in and through Christ, of the ultimate triumph and victory of all human endeavours to follow the good. Here is a message of hope and confidence in the outcome of the moral struggle; a conviction that 'God works together all things for good to them that love him[6]'. The evidence for this is in the Resurrection of Christ after the Crucifixion of Good Friday, in the emergence of the Christian Church from a group of dejected disciples. The Christian view is that Easter Day was a turning of the tide, a turning point in the affairs of men. From that time, no matter how long the haul, no matter how troublesome the journey, no matter what the backslidings, the difficulties, the frustrations, victory ultimately is assured. Just as in a long war there may be some event, after which the end of the war cannot be in doubt whatever be the intervening campaigns, so with the future of humanity. After the first Easter Day we know that the purposes of God will ultimately triumph, and that the last word will be with that redeeming love which we know in Christ.

This does not mean that the Christian expects moral difficulties and problems to disappear overnight. Not only because we are much more sensitive, but because of practical and technological progress our moral problems seem often harder than ever. Those who put their trust in some kind of moral code begin not surprisingly to wonder whether any moral code could ever be devised to grapple effectively with problems of this intricacy and complexity and the result is either moral apathy or moral despair. Our society displays both possibilities. But beset with the same complexities and puzzles the Christian remembers that at the moment of greatest triumph, Christ on the Cross thought that he was forsaken. The Christian is a stark realist — facing the facts no matter how many or how unpleasant, and yet going forward in confidence and hope that moral insights will prevail and that the good will ultimately triumph. In other words, he has a conviction about morality, and the significance of morality, that the mere possession of a moral code could never give him.

I realise of course that this kind of reflection soon expands into convictions about life after death, whereas the question from which we started explicitly excludes that topic. But that remark is only meant to show that at least the Christian faith is of a piece, and through and through coherent.

An adequate morality which has both the inwardness necessary for genuine morality, the power to survive repeated moral failure, and the ability to face facts, however unpleasant, and the possibility of constant reform, points beyond any moral code to a person and to a religious dimension as a necessary supplement. This is what Christianity has to offer. This is not to say that any and every way of relating religion and morality has to be accepted. For instance, religion should not be seen as giving some kind of sanctions to morality, providing reasons of a non-moral kind for doing good actions. Such sanctions would be destructive of genuine morality, they would conflict with what is rightly called the 'autonomy of morals'. We must not do good, for example, 'for the sake of everlasting happiness'. We must do good as a spontaneous response to a moral claim that inspires us.

At the same time, we may agree with the philosopher Kant that nevertheless an Ideal which united duty and happiness would be something better than an Ideal confined to duty itself and, said Kant in effect, we may think of the idea of God as something which does justice to this particular insight, and brings greater coherence into our moral thinking and reasoning. In short, religion, and Christianity in particular, gives a wider setting to morality. It links morality and nature, the 'ought' and the 'is' without compromising the 'autonomy of morals'.

I have tried, then, to argue that what Christianity has to offer to someone who has his own moral code is something needed by all moral codes if they are to lead to genuine morality; something needed if we are to face all the facts including some of the most unpleasant ones about ourselves; and something needed if we wish to have a coherent view of the whole universe, in which morality is only one area of human existence, albeit an area of the highest possible significance and importance.

IAN DUNELM:

[1] Exod. 20:9,10,12–17 *(New English Bible)*
[2] Rom. 7:7–8.
[3] Rom. 7:19.
[4] Rom. 7:15.
[5] Deut. 5:14 and 21.
[6] A variant translation of Rom. 8:28.

What place has individual conscience in Christianity?

Before we attempt to answer this question, we must pause for a moment to ask what we mean by 'conscience'. Of course, we are all familiar with the word, and also with those experiences to which the word refers. Yet if we consider how we talk about conscience, we soon realize that we are discussing something that is far from simple.

Consider the following sentences: 'My conscience tells me that I should not oppose an increase in taxes, because more money is needed for public services'; 'His conscience has been troubling him since he voted against the measure'; 'He followed his conscience, but he was wrong in what he did'.

In the first of these sentences, the word 'conscience' stands for a faculty of judgment. We all have to decide between different courses of action that may be open to us, and the decision depends to some extent on the moral question of what is right and what is wrong. Conscience is our capacity to discriminate between right and wrong, good and bad. We have a capacity for moral discernment, just as we have a capacity to discern between true and false or between beautiful and ugly. Thus, in our first sentence, conscience is understood as part of that complex mental apparatus which is ours in virtue of the fact that we are thinking, reasonable, responsible beings.

In the second of our three sentences, the word 'conscience' is used somewhat differently. It no longer refers to a course of action which still lies ahead and is to be chosen, but to something which has already been done. In this case, conscience is not a capacity for judgment so much as a feeling or emotion. It is a feeling of pain or uneasiness, where we have done something which, either at the time of acting or later, conflicts with our standards of right and wrong; or occasionally it may be a feeling of satisfaction, where we have overcome the temptation to do something that was wrong or dubious, and have chosen what we believed to be the right course. Most of us are better acquainted with an uneasy conscience (a so-called 'bad conscience') than with a satisfied one; and if we feel too often satisfied with what we have done, this may be simply the smugness and complacency associated with an insensitive conscience.

Our third sentence, which talks of someone following his conscience and still being wrong, reminds us that conscience is not infallible. Even if conscience is in some sense a God-given faculty, it is not simply 'the voice of God' within us. This voice is always filtered through some human medium. In a world in which sin is a reality, even conscience can be distorted and we persuade ourselves that our own desires are also God's commands.

But need we bring God into the discussion at all? Can we not say that conscience is just a part of man's nature, like his instincts and his other powers, and that it does not, either directly or indirectly, derive from God or from any reality beyond man himself?

Freud elaborated a well-known theory of conscience as the super-ego, a kind of built-in mechanism which represses anti-social behaviour. In our early childhood, we are forcibly prevented by parents and teachers from engaging in such behaviour. Their standards 'rub off' on us, so to speak, and when the parents or teachers are no longer around to deter us from undesirable actions, a part of our own psyche, the so-called 'super-ego', has become conditioned to act in their stead and to monitor our conduct.

Freud's theory obviously does account for part of what we understand by conscience. Clearly, however, it is the more negative aspects of conscience that he has in view, especially the pain and guilt-feeling which we experience after doing something which goes against the conventional standards of the society in which we have been brought up. But Freud's theory fails to account for the more constructive and forward-looking functions of conscience. Furthermore, he fails to explain how there could ever have been moral progress in the history of mankind. If, in that history, each generation has tended to take over uncritically the standards of the preceding generation and to feel guilt when these standards are violated, it is also true to say that in this same history individuals or groups of individuals have occasionally rebelled against the standards of the parents, and they have done this in the name of conscience. In other words, the conscience of an individual or of a group of individuals may sometimes clash with the inherited morality of the super-ego, and this proves that conscience is more than the super-ego. Slavery would still be with us if there had not been some individuals whose consciences burst out of the conventional morality of their parents. Perhaps war will end in the same way, namely when a generation arrives that will conscientiously reject the values of earlier generations, so far as these allowed war as an instrument of policy. A part — though one must say, *only* a part — of the current revolt of American youth is due to the dissatisfaction of many young people with the accepted moral standards of the affluent society of their parents. The idealism of youth is therefore one very important manifestation of conscience which cannot be accounted for in terms of the super-ego.

Actually, Freud himself became aware of the inadequacy of the super-ego theory to account for the complex idea of conscience, and in his later writings he introduced the notion of the 'ego ideal'. His followers have developed this notion to a considerably further extent. The ego ideal tries to take account of the constructive, forward-looking, creative aspects of conscience, as distinct from the repressive and negative aspects of the super-ego. Everyone projects into the future an image or an ideal towards which he aspires. This ideal guides our conduct, and following it will sometimes bring us into conflict with the deliverances of the super-ego itself. But when we talk in this way, we are recognizing that man is more than the mere natural phenomenon or mechanistic psyche which the classical Freudian model represented him to be.

Let me now try to state a Christian theory of conscience which will make central those creative and forward-looking aspects which Freud introduced only as an afterthought, but which will also try to hold on to Freud's realism and recognize that much of what we take to be the voice of conscience may be only the voice of a conventional wisdom.

We begin with the teaching that man was created in the image of God. What does this mean? Surely each one of us is limited and finite, in his power, his knowledge and every other respect. How then can we be said to have any likeness to God?

The likeness lies in our freedom and creativity. We are not just parts of the world but have the power to act in the world and to change it. We can build up the world in such a way that at the same time we build up our own humanity. This would mean that we would become more fully persons, more fully like God himself. For to say that we are created in the image of God does not mean that we have been fashioned according to some predetermined pattern, as a manufactured article is produced according to specifications laid down in advance. The image of

God is a potentiality within man and it may be either realized or lost. This follows from the fact that it consists of freedom and creativity. These are not fixed properties, like the colour of one's eyes or hair. Freedom and creativity are possibilities which only become real as we exercise them.

Furthermore, the exercise of freedom and creativity is inseparable from risk. If we are free to build up the world, this implies that we are also free to destroy it. Our present concern over the deterioration of the environment, the pollution of the air, the rivers and the oceans, the wasteful destruction of plant and animal life, is a sad reminder that we abuse our freedom and that our creative powers are often diverted from building a world fit for a community of persons to devising ways of making a quick profit and of securing a selfish advantage without regard to how this will effect other people.

Yet that image in which we are created is never obliterated. We do indeed talk of original sin, and by that we mean the corporate disorder of humanity which distorts all human striving and diminishes our true personhood. Yet however original and deeply rooted sin may be, the goodness of creation is even more original. God made the world good and he gave his image to man — this is the first and basic teaching of the Bible about creation. Sin comes along subsequently, and it could not be otherwise, for sin is essentially negative and parasitic in its nature. The very fact that we are aware of sin shows that we are not wholly destroyed by it. Deep within us, the image, in which we were created and for which we are destined, remains, even if it has been obscured. It still points us in the direction of a full personhood. It points us towards freedom, creativity, love, joy, peace — all the things that are positive and that make our lives more truly human and personal as well as more like God, who brings all these qualities to perfection. The image always goes ahead of us, as it were, drawing us beyond ourselves, opening up new dimensions of selfhood, promoting our growth. That image is our conscience, our deep-down awareness of who we are meant to be and who we ought to be. And every time we turn away from it, we experience the pain of violating that which lies at the very foundation of our being. The pain of conscience is the very real pain of a diminished self. It is the pain experienced when, instead of growing and becoming more fully personal, we have rather shrunk and slipped back to a lower level.

I have said that sin never totally obliterates the image in which man was made. If it did, we would no longer have a conscience and we would be unaware of our sinful condition. But in saying these things, I have no wish to minimize the effects of sin. No one who has lived in the twentieth century, through the horrors and holocausts that have stained the years of this century, can close his eyes to the fact that the divine image in man has been disfigured to the point of almost disappearing, and that human conscience has grown so weak that it cannot prevent the greatest evils from breaking out. Thus, while I have mentioned the Biblical doctrine of creation to explain the foundation of conscience, I must go on to the specifically Christian doctrine of redemption. Among other things, Jesus Christ has restored and quickened the conscience of man. If every man is a bearer of the divine image, however disfigured it may have become, Jesus Christ is the one for whom it is uniquely claimed that he is the 'express image' of God (Heb. 1:3). He has gone ahead of the rest of mankind (the same Epistle to the Hebrews calls him a 'pioneer' or 'forerunner') so as to realize in its fulness that perfect personhood for which all were destined in creation. This means, however, that he is not only the express image of God, but also the measure of a perfect humanity or mature manhood (Eph. 4:13). The knowledge of who we are and where we should be going, given to us in creation as the image of God but then obscured by sin, is restored in Christ, so that he becomes, as it were, the conscience of mankind. St. Athanasius suggested that it was as if a portrait had long ago been painted on a panel of wood. That portrait had gradually faded and decayed. But now the subject himself returns, not merely in a picture but as a living presence, to renew the image in all mankind.

But although we think of Christ as the measure or pattern of a true humanity and although we sometimes speak of the 'imitation' of Christ, we should realize that, just as in the case of the image of God in men, this does not mean that all must conform to a fixed model. Christ opens up for us the direction in which man must go to become fully man, but there are many possible ways of following Christ — as many, perhaps, as there are unique human individuals in the world. Following Christ does not mean a copycat imitation of his life which, after all, was lived under very different historical conditions from the ones we know. It means rather the intelligent and conscientious attempt to express the spirit of Christ (the spirit of love, freedom, creativity) in the world of the twentieth century. Christ himself is always disclosing something new. There is an inexhaustibility in the Lord of the Church. His total meaning was not fully grasped by the first disciples, nor by the next generation or the next again. Even today, we are still finding new light and guidance for life in Jesus Christ.

Does the fact that the Christian conscience has been enlightened by Jesus Christ set the Christian apart from non-Christians in his understanding of the duties of the moral life? I think this question must be answered both Yes and No. If indeed Christ is the 'express image' of God and if he renews the image of God in his followers, then these followers have received a new understanding of who they are and who they ought to be, and this understanding differentiates them from those in whom the image of God has been eroded by sin and never renewed. But we should understand that this is not some privilege of the Christian about which he could feel himself superior. It is rather a tremendous responsibility that is laid upon him — an almost frightening responsibility, were not Christ the source of grace in human life, as well as the standard by which that life is to be measured.

The early Christians did think of themselves as separated from the world, and Christ warned them that the world would mercilessly persecute them. Often in these early centuries Christian conscience bore witness against the world even to the point of death, as, for instance, when Christians refused to pay divine homage to the Emperor. It was that fearless witness of conscience which led many pagans to perceive the renewal of humanity that was taking place in the Church, so that they too came into its ranks. Right down to our own days, there are occasions when Christian conscience must bring us into conflict with the standards and practices of pagan or secularized societies.

But there is another side to the picture, and this too has been recognized since the earliest times. Outside of the Church, one often meets good, generous, concerned people whose devotion to high ideals would put many Christians to shame. St. Paul knew good pagans. He wrote: 'When Gentiles who have not the law do what the law requires, they are a law to themselves, even though they do not have the law. They show that what the law requires is written on their hearts, while their conscience also bears witness and their conflicting thoughts accuse or perhaps excuse them' (Rom. 2:14—15). If we have been right in connecting conscience with the image of God, then conscience is found in all humanity, for that image is never quite abolished. Furthermore, it was that same image which Christ renewed and brought to a new level. Thus there is a fundamental affinity between the conscience of

the Christian and the conscience of many a serious-minded person
outside of the Church, whether he professes another religion or
even no religion at all. Theologians have used the expression
'natural law' for these profound moral convictions which we all
share.

Thus the Christian is not always in conflict with the world.
Sometimes, quite unexpectedly, he will find allies among those
who do not share his faith. This is important in the world today,
where Christians are often a small minority and where they
cannot hope to achieve very much by 'going it alone' in the battle
against such vast social evils as war, racial discrimination,
exploitation and the like. In these matters, the Christian must be
prepared to join hands with others not of his faith whose
consciences have become aroused and who, because of the law
'written on their hearts', may be as much committed as the
Christian in the crusade for a world better fitted to allow for the
growth of personal selves in a community of respect and good
will.

So the Christian's attitude to the world is not a simple one,
but a discriminating one. He must know when to make his
conscientious witness against the evils of the world, but he must
know too how to recognize and co-operate with everything that is
good in the world and that is following out the healthful
directions toward which man was directed when he was created in
the image of God.

If the individual's conscience has to be discriminating with
regard to the world, the same is true with regard to the Church.
Does it seem surprising to say this? Would not conscience bid us
obey and support the Church? I am sure that for most of the time
it certainly would. But no human institutions are perfect and
even if the Church, as the mystery of Christ's Body, is more than
a human institution, nevertheless it has its all-too-human side.
Sometimes individual Christians, in obedience to their
consciences, have had to stand up against the Church itself. This
was true of Luther, when he declared that he could do no other
than follow the path he had chosen. The Church always needs
some courageous people who are prepared to challenge it from
within. Only so can it be saved from complacency and even from
corruption and be a Church *semper reformanda* – in constant
process of being remade. The Church especially needs its young
people, with their freshness of vision, to challenge its accepted
ways and to drive it to conscientious reflection.

Yet if conscience ever compels us to challenge the accepted

ways or to depart from the commonly accepted moral standards, we should not do this with arrogance or self-righteousness, but with humility and even, I may say, with fear and trembling. I think that today there are many conscientious people, but I am sometimes appalled that some of them are so utterly convinced of their own rightness that they cannot listen to anyone else. No conscience is utterly pure or completely enlightened. The great eighteenth-century philosopher, Bishop Butler, was a champion of conscience and regarded it as the highest of human faculties. But in his sermon on Balaam, he showed how even a good conscientious man can manipulate his conscience so that it counsels him to do just what he wants. None of us are free from this danger. No person should ever be forced to act against his conscience, and we should not try to silence the conscience of anyone who believes that he has to speak out against Church or State or conventional morality. But everyone who takes it upon himself to do that has a duty to search and prove his conscience. He must be prepared to listen to those who differ from him. He must be prepared to open his heart to the counsel of his friends. If he is a Christian, he must seek by prayer and study to let his conscience be formed and enlightened by Christ.

In sum, conscience is a great gift, the very stamp of our origin from God. We rejoice that all men partake of this gift, and that we can conscientiously join with them in every course of action that promotes the well-being of God's creatures. We rejoice even more that Jesus Christ has renewed the faded image and become the pioneer of conscience, opening the way toward a new creation.

JOHN MACQUARRIE

Doesn't the teaching of Jesus, e.g., the Sermon on the Mount, make it impossible to be a Christian today?

On one of the occasions when Dr. Siegmund-Schultze, the distinguished German sociologist, was court-martialled on account of his pacifist attitude during the First World War, he was only saved from the death-sentence by producing a letter from the Kaiser in which occurred this sentence: 'Dr. Schultze's attitude is only Christianity, but it is not possible to live Christianity now.'

This quotation raises at a particular point of debate what is clearly a fundamental general question about the teaching of Jesus. It may be put thus: in the end, when we have been as honest as we can about the whole matter, is the Sermon on the Mount to be regarded as no more than a sublime narrative of heaven, a kind of romance of religion and morals in the pages of which we may lose ourselves now and again with pleasure and profit, but from which we must return at the call of hard, irreducible fact — no doubt purer and blither in spirit for breathing that mountain air — but return all the same to make terms with the grim world of reality? Or is it intended to be a programme of action for transforming the world? 'Judge not that ye be not judged', said Christ. Is this hard saying which robs us of a subtle luxury — the luxury of self-justification by dint of clever criticizing — is this hard saying a description of the life of the angels, or is it an indispensable method of making bad men good? 'Resist not evil . . . love your enemies', said Christ. Are these to be taken as counsels of perfection which we may begin to think of applying to life when there is not much evil left to resist, and not many enemies left to fight, or do they constitute a sober and serious policy for overcoming evil and turning enemies into friends? 'Be ye perfect even as your Father which is in heaven is perfect', said Christ. Will anyone but a fantastic fool, or that still less admirable creature, the youthful prig, venture to include such a precept in his working kit for life upon the earth?

I know of no questions to which I should rather see students applying themselves with earnestness than just such questions, for until they have faced Jesus Christ upon the plane of his moral demands, they have not faced him seriously at all. No cut and dry answer can be given to questions like these, for like all the deepest questions of life, they belong to a realm in which the individual must arrive at his own personal answer, must register his vote under God's inviolable rule of secret balloting, and must pay in his own body and destiny the price of the vote he gives. All I seek here to do is to present three considerations which are relevant to the question at issue and which ought to be before the mind of any man who is honestly facing the moral demand of Christ.

First, there is a plain fact of history. It is easier to live Christianity today than it has ever been in the world's history, and that because in past ages some men have judged it possible to do it and tried it. By far the most frequent objection which is made today to the Christian moralist or evangelist runs something like this. 'We admire Jesus Christ. We hold him to be the greatest teacher that has ever lived. But we belong to a "system" which is fundamentally unchristian, and in which, therefore, we have no fair chance of living the Christian life. Change the system, and then come back to us with your Christian message, and we shall give you a warmer welcome.' No one need deny the elements of truth in a position like that. We do live in a system which is deeply unchristian, in which sentence I am not referring to any particular economic or political organization, but to what St. John calls 'the whole world which lies in the power of the evil one'. But what does need to be denied in a position like the one outlined is the implied premiss that things were once otherwise, in the sense that they were once more favourable to the working out of Christianity. They were never otherwise in that sense, least of all in that Roman world into which Christ sent out his first disciples as 'sheep among wolves'. If it is hard to live Christianity today, it was harder when a Nero or a Domitian ruled the world. The truth is that in two thousand years, as system has replaced system, something of the gentleness of Christ has crept into the organized life of mankind, something of his teaching become incorporate in their institutions; and the leavening force in that transformation has always been one and the same — men and women who did not think it ridiculous to pray, 'Thy will be done in earth as it is in heaven', and who strove to match their lives to their prayers. No one can ever again be bolder than St. Peter or St. Paul. The gentler mood of the world, a civilization partially watered from the springs of Christ, admits of no repetition of the

courage of the pioneers. If, then, we must evade the daunting
demands of Jesus, let us at least not do it on the false plea that
we have a less good chance of conforming to them than others
have had in past times.

A second relevant consideration belongs to the realm of faith.
The ethics of the Sermon on the Mount are not set forth as an
abstract law which is essentially alien to the world in which we
live, but in the context of, and in inseparable relation with, a
religious faith about the world in which we live. In other words,
the ethical demand of Christ is the corollary in action of a
theology. It is a demand made upon the will upon the basis of a
belief about the constitution and manner of coherence of this
very world of ours. The ultimate sanction of the Sermon on the
Mount is nothing else but this — the faith that our world is
actually being governed consistently with these principles, and
only hangs together because it is so governed. Behind the ethical
demand is the faith that the sovereign God is loving his enemies,
is sending down sun and rain upon just and unjust, is not resisting
evil as violent men resist evil, is doing at all times and in all places
his pure and perfect will. We are thus summoned, not to clamber
laboriously and heave ourselves painfully up to some unnaturally
high platform of life, like climbers who, to scale some towering
peak, must leave far behind the fertile valleys and pastoral
foothills of their native home, but rather to dig down where we
stand through sand and mud in order to find the rock of reality
and a firm foundation for civilization beneath our very feet. And
thus, too, when we fail to conform to the moral demand of
Christ, we may not pity ourselves as baffled idealists, haunted by
a dream of perfection which continually goes to wreck on the
grim reefs of reality; still less may we congratulate ourselves on
being rather wonderful creatures to have dreamed so fair a dream;
we must rather condemn ourselves as rebels — rebels against the
very constitution and government of the world.

This conviction belongs, as I have said, to the realm of faith,
and is therefore not capable of coercive demonstration. Of
course, there is much in the world which appears to contradict
it — so much that some modern moralists give up belief in God
altogether, although at the same time trying to save from the
wreck the precious casket of Christ's teaching. About this and
any other such attempt to retain Christ's ethics while discarding
his theology, two comments may fairly be made. When you have
carved out Christ's ethics from his theology, the thing you have
left on your hands is not a dead theology and a living ethic, but a

dead theology and a dead ethic. You murder to dissect. Christ is no mere ethical teacher propounding a new law; he is a Saviour offering a new life on the basis of reconciliation with the living God, and on that basis alone. Meanwhile we may remind ourselves that a humanist church is no new idea. It was tried nearly two hundred years ago in France, and when it did not greatly succeed, when, indeed, it could already be described as a bleak failure, one of its leaders went to Talleyrand to confide his disappointment and obtain the sagacious ex-bishop's advice. 'There is one plan which you might at least try,' said Talleyrand. 'I should recommend you to be crucified, and to rise again the third day!'

Jesus Christ does not torture the conscience of men by propounding a formidable ethic without offering an equivalent dynamic, and that is the specific feature of his ethical scheme.

That leads me to the third consideration which ought to be before anyone who is facing in any serious spirit the moral demands of Christ. It belongs to the realm of morals itself and may be presented thus. Whatever may have been their relation in geography, the Mount of the Sermon and the Mount of the Crucifixion are twin-peaks in the landscape of life.

At certain times it would be a relief if we could forget the bloodstained Cross of Christ. Most of all, at those times when, in one or another context of practical living, it has become plain that, if the will of God is to be done on earth as it is done in heaven, we ourselves, since we belong to a system which lies in the power of the evil one, must do that will in our own spirits and bodies, and pay the price of suffering which is for ever imaged in the death of Jesus. It would be indeed a relief to forget the Cross then, for then we might fall back upon the comparatively distinguished role of baffled idealist, and make our skilful compromises with a show of dignity, and manage to stifle in our souls the hateful, haunting charge of cowardice. That is what men do who separate the Mount of the Sermon from the Mount of the Crucifixion, and, whether they know it or not, their motive for making the separation is to justify their doing it.

Is it not simply true that the natural man in us, which is the sinful man in us, wants the lands and the houses and all the other good things without the persecutions? And is it not also true that Jesus Christ has never deceived men about the primary condition of discipleship and never abates it? It is this: 'Take up your cross, and follow me.'

A. C. CRAIG

What is wrong with the 'Permissive Society'?

The phrase 'The Permissive Society' implies two things of which I don't think those who use the phrase are very often aware or remember. The first implication is that permission is being granted; in other words that there are certain rules, but permission is being given for exceptions to those rules. The second implication is that there is somebody who is giving permission, somebody who is as it were extending the latitude of the rules a little bit more widely than perhaps in the past they've been allowed to extend.

Now who gives the permission? I think we might all agree on the following description of our society and our moral condition in the West; that, first, over the last fifty years or so there has been simultaneously an increasing disbelief in God, and secondly, that there's been a decline in the acceptance (not necessarily in the practice) of traditional Western moral values. I don't think that anybody could deny that is an accurate description of our situation. But the differences begin when one interprets that description.

Now there are two very different interpretations of the situation we are in. First of all there is the position of what I should call religious morality and according to this these two facts are closely connected together. The loss of belief in God and a rejection of moral values follow from each other, so that you can't have one without the other. This is a popular theme of pulpits up and down the land, but it also has quite respectable representatives. Dostoevsky is a very respectable member of this team as it were, and in *The Brothers Karamazov* he gives us the character of Ivan who holds that if God does not exist then *tout est permis* — anything goes. There's no reason why one should not steal or murder. Nikita was quite clear that after the death of God it would be futile for people to think that they can hang on to the moral sense that God has so to speak bequeathed to us on his deathbed. Nikita was quite clear that you can't think that belief in God can go, with man going quietly on holding and obeying the same moral codes as before. This view suggests that there is a close connection between the decline in morals or beliefs about morals and the decline in the belief of God. But there's a second interpretation — what one might call the view of secular morality. This is also highly respectable and its proponents would say something like this. Those who used to believe in God as we no longer do believed in a good God and after all isn't there something in this? You often hear people say as an expletive 'Good God', but you never hear anyone saying 'Bad God'. Why is this? The implication is that people believe in a good God rather than a revengeful, tyrannical God or a seriously immoral God. This means that they have a notion of good which they apply to God, and which is therefore independent of God. So, when people no longer believe in God, they can still go on having this independent moral sense; and indeed the secular moralist will go on to say that it is even more moral if it is independent of the notion of God. On the old view, he would say, God was used as a kind of big stick, an external threat to make people behave properly or to punish them if they didn't. And, says the secular moralist, now that we've abolished God people can be good not for external reasons but because of their own true inner moral sense; indeed it's more moral to do right for right's sake than just because of threats and rewards. And so these people say that what we call the secular decline in traditional moral values is actually an advance because it's an acceptance of what is right because it's right, and not just because society or parents or teachers, or still less a God, dictate it to us from outside. And this, they say, is a more responsible sense of right and wrong. It is technically called by philosophers 'the autonomy of morals', morals that we give to ourselves rather than something merely conventional, traditional, external or theological.

These, then, are the two views very roughly put. These are the two interpretations of what we agreed about our present society. What is to be our own view of these two interpretations? I think that the first thing that needs saying (and I think it needs saying especially in view of the fact that many Christians are beginning to panic a little about the permissive society from which I started) is that there are certain initial misunderstandings which need to be cleared up about these two views, that is to say, the secular moral view and the religious moral view. The first is that the secular moralists often get us Christians wrong. They accuse us of a kind of ethics of tyranny, they say that we only do our duty because God shakes his big stick up at us. But in fact the central Christian tradition does not accept this, indeed it rejects the very idea of an ethics of tyranny. Conscience must always in the last resort be followed. Surely that means that Christians also hold an autonomous ethic, that is, an ethic which we must apply for ourselves. The responsibility is on the individual, no man can be forced to do right, it must be his own choice. That's why it's perfectly possible for Christians to say, 'You must love the sinner even though you hate the sin.' That's why it's always been accepted that there's a distinction between what we call 'subjectively right' and 'objectively wrong'. For example, a sincere and well-adjusted cannibal who opposes anti-social behaviour will of course eat his enemies in the correct manner because this is part of the pattern of his society. We may believe that cannibalism is objectively wrong; but we can't deny that, given his code, he is behaving subjectively right. In other words he's obeying his conscience in eating his enemies because this is what he's been taught to believe is right.

There is more to it than that. The central Christian tradition also believes that there is a wide sphere of duty (that is, of moral behaviour) which has nothing to do necessarily and directly with religion at all. St. Paul implies this when he taught that there are certain natural laws of right and wrong which don't need any special revelation. Men are born with them, they're already there in the hearts of heathen people. That's why even though they know nothing of God in Christ yet 'they have no excuse' for their immorality because 'their own hearts condemn them'. There have been different ways of expressing this truth. One of the ways which is now regarded as rather old-fashioned is the doctrine of a Natural Law. Unfortunately some of the representatives of Natural Law have not done it the best kind of service. Sometimes the use made of this idea of Natural Law has been so vague that it's unhelpful; and sometimes it has been so precise that in fact it can't be applied. I think that the idea of a Natural Law which is shared by all people, not just Christians, and which comprises duty, so to speak, without necessarily bringing in deity at all, is very important indeed. After all, it is implied in the charter of the United Nations about human rights, and it's important because it does mean that we can recognize certain universal rules of conduct by which we can judge any one civilization. In other words, if law is only what one civilization decides shall be law, then we have no right to stand in judgement upon another civilization, and we could say that the Nazi rules were perfectly valid rules because they were passed in valid Nazi courts and we would have no right to say those Nazi rules were wrong. It's only if we can appeal to something that is above particular nations, something that is universal and natural to man as such that we can make any condemnation, or indeed any moral comparison of one society or another.

So when non-Christians, the secular moralists, say to us Christians 'Why should you try to impose your moral system on a nation when you're only a minority, as all the figures show?' surely our reply must be, 'Please be precise: to which moral systems do you refer? Are you referring to Western law generally?' It's true that we grew up in a Christian civilization but a great deal of it is common to mankind as such. And in claiming that this is the right law for mankind, we are not just defending a Christian moral law, we are defending man himself, we are concerned to preserve man himself. The Ten Commandments for instance say, 'Thou shalt not steal' but in fact you don't necessarily need a command from God in order to be able to deduce the quite obvious logical fact that if there were no rule against stealing there could be no such thing as stealing at all, because there would be no such thing as property, there would be no thine or mine, and therefore there would be no reason why anybody should steal or why it would be wrong to do so. So, you see, on this view there's a great deal of morals which are common not only to the great religions of the world and Christianity but also to secular morality. And therefore there's an area of duty in which deity is not directly concerned.

But you may say that in view of the whole history of Christian tradition, surely there must be some difference. Why should it be that there is a whole set of moral problems which are particular to the Christian? Does the existence of God make all that difference to what we ought to do? Is there a little bit of something extra which, as it were, others haven't got?

I would suggest very briefly that there are three areas of difference. The first is that while in fact Christians believe that we share certain duties in common with non-Christians, we are peculiar in saying that though man has these duties he doesn't perform them. This is the 'gloomy Christian doctrine of original sin' as the secular moralists call it, although why it's gloomy I have never been able to understand, except perhaps in the obvious sense in which we say the weather man is being gloomy about the weather prospects on T.V. If that's gloom I would rather have gloom and truth than build up hopes of a fine picnic which are going to be falsified. And Christians say if you really rely on man to do what is right in his own strength and by the use of unaided reason then that is likely to lead to far gloomier results because you'll find yourself let down again and again. That's the big difference. And secondly, there is the fact that there is a difference in quality in what Christians believe. Although Christians share a great deal in common with non-Christians, yet the fact that Christians believe that what we do here has important significance for man's eternal destiny does add something extra.

And this leads to the third difference that the religious morals make and this is the fact that duty is not everything. It does not comprise the whole of man's behaviour. William Blake, that very extraordinary, heretical, strange, but very gifted prophetic poet said, 'If Christianity is morals then Socrates was the Saviour.' I believe that it's only in a sense deity that is able to put duty in its right place, because duty simply pursued for its own sake can turn a man into a legalistic and moralistic being who is thinking all the time 'How much have I got to do and how little need I do and get away with it?' But a Christian man believes he must do his duty not just because it is his duty but for God's sake. In a sense our loyalty to a true and loving God leads us to do our duty and more than our duty. It leads us to be ready not only exactly to pay what we owe but to give ourselves, to go the extra mile, to turn the other cheek. All these parabolic phrases of our Lord imply that man is more than someone who just as it were balances his books and keeps them straight. This is finally brought out in that great parable of our Lord where he says that when we as Christians are considering our duty to our neighbour and when we look at our neighbour and see how we behave to our neighbour, we should treat our neighbour with even more care and even more compassion if behind our neighbour's face we see something of the image of God himself. You remember the parable: 'In as much as ye did it — either right or wrong — unto the least of these my brethren — or my children — ye did it unto me.'

MARTIN JARRETT-KERR, C.R.

When you look at the Christian Church, there is probably much there that shocks you; and no wonder. Through the centuries men and women have looked at the Christian Church and they have been shocked. There is the claim of a divine message and a divine life, the claim of the Church to be representing Jesus Christ in the world; and yet so many things are there that don't look Christian at all. That has always been so. It is so today, and there is a sense in which it may be so until the end of time. The Christian Church consists of fallible and sinful men and women and children whom God chooses to use for his great purpose.

Now the Christian Church has many titles, and one of its most striking descriptions is 'the Body of Christ'. What does that mean? Well, there is a terrible literalness about it. It means that, just as Jesus when he lived in Galilee and Jerusalem had a body of flesh and bones and blood through which he lived and worked and showed himself to the world, so now after the Resurrection Jesus, though out of sight, still has again a body through which he lives and works, and carries out his purpose in the world. And that body is now composed of the lives of baptized Christian men and women and children. 'Ye are the body of Christ', St. Paul says to the Christians of his own day; and the words are still true, truly addressed to us who are Christians today. 'Ye are the body of Christ', the family fellowship of those who with Christ and in Christ and through Christ are called to worship God in depth, and who by their worship are proclaiming the priority of God in the world. They are called to carry the message of divine love brought by Christ to the world, and to serve humanity in the name of Christ. And that body of Christ, that society, is composed of the divine fact of Christ's forgiveness and Christ's life — 'Peace be unto you', — and also by the human fact of horribly fallible and weak Christian men and women.

Now besides the description 'body of Christ', there is another significant description, 'saints', 'called to be saints'. Those terms are applied to all Christians, and they did not mean, and they do not mean, that a member of the Church is always perfect. No. But they do mean that a member of the Church has received the Holy Spirit, the spirit of saintliness, and is thus put in the way of becoming truly saintly and reflecting the very love and life of Christ. Called to be saints — that's the description of all the members of the Church. But within that calling there are many varieties. There are those who have so yielded themselves to the power of Christ's spirit that they are saints indeed, actually reflecting the very love of Christ in themselves. There are those who are able authentically to submit themselves to the power of Christ's Spirit, and are on the way towards it; a way marked by a deep humility and penitence and sense of unworthiness. There are those who only very spasmodically and fitfully put themselves in that way, perhaps at certain times and not at others, with the great danger that to be concerned about it sometimes and not at others is to risk soon not being concerned about it at all. And there are also those who, while within the institution of the Christian Church, are frankly conventional and not taking their responsibility with any seriousness.

The Christian Church was then, and the Christian Church is now, this mixed body of those called to be saints. There is glory, the spirit of God whereby saints are created; there is scandal, the very inadequate and fitful response which many of us who are members make. Well, that is our situation as a Church, and as members of the Church. But to understand it further there are certain things that we must bear in mind.

First, all of us who are Christians are equally involved in the Church's scandal, and any sort of 'we' and 'they' talk is excluded by a right understanding of the matter. If you were the Archbishop of Canterbury, anything silly or wicked that you did would do a great deal of damage to the witness of the Christian Church. You can imagine what people would say, and what would happen if you were the Archbishop of Canterbury, and your folly and your sin would do big culpable public damage to the Christian Church and to the Christian cause. But if you are not the Archbishop of Canterbury, then be very sure that you by your folly and your sinfulness and unworthiness as a Christian can be doing to Christ, the Church, and yourself, and to the Christian cause, just as much great damage. That must be realized. What is your calling? Jesus said, 'I am the vine, ye are the branches.' That's you. Jesus said 'By this shall all men know that ye are my disciples, if ye love one another.' That's you. The Apostle says, 'Ye are the body of Christ.' That's you. It means that every single one of you by inconsistency with that profession can be doing damage than which no damage is greater, for God alone knows whether his Church and his truth is the more damaged by big public scandals or by the more secret scandalous behaviour of any one of us. And indeed the damage that you do by your inconsistency to your own soul, a soul created by God in God's own image, can be terrible. Above all the wound that you can administer by your inconsistency to Christ, a member of whose body you are, cannot be exaggerated. One of the apostolic writers said that the inconsistencies of Christians crucify the Son of God afresh. That is a description of the inconsistency of any of us Christians in any office or in no office, public or private, crucifying the Son of God afresh by not being like a member of his body and a branch of his vine. The scandal of the Church is the scandal of everyone who bears the name of Christ, and all matters of 'we' and 'they' and 'he' have to be done away in facing the facts under the only light that truly discloses them to us, namely the light that falls from the Cross of Christ.

As the scandal is the scandal of us all, so too the glory of Christ in his Church is a glory that can be known anywhere and everywhere. Let me give you an illustration of misunderstanding about this. Recently I was in a university where some of the Christian students were telling me about a superb effort that some of them were making to run a plan in their great city to enable the better housing of quite a number of its citizens. A wonderful piece of practical Christian work! One of them said to me rather angrily, 'Yes, we are doing this; but why doesn't the Church do something about it?' I had to tell these dear people 'Ye are the body of Christ.' It is the glory of the Church that you are doing that. What they really meant by 'Why doesn't the Church do something about it? was 'Why doesn't the Archbishop of Canterbury pay attention and make a speech about it?' As if that can do any good to anybody at all! 'Ye are the body of Christ' and there, in that city, there were those Christian students — they were not pagans, they were baptized Christians saying their prayers, living by the life of Christ and his Holy Spirit — doing this great piece of Christian service, really being the body of Christ. The glory and the scandal are diffused in every single member of the Church.

There is a second principle that can help us: history shows that attempts to be rid of the scandal of the Church by puritanically turning out of the Church people who don't conform to certain moral standards cause more evils than they cure. The Church is a mixed society of those called to be saints, baptized in the Spirit, and with very very mixed responses within it. Now again and again the sense of scandal of the Church having so many passengers in it has led to movements ancient, mediaeval, post-reformation, which have said in effect: 'Let's turn out of the Church people who don't conform to certain high moral standards.' Usually it has taken the form of turning out the fornicators, turning out anybody who has lapsed in respect of sexual morality, and defining the Church as the coterie of those who really do live up to a certain moral standard. Attempts to purge the Church like that break down because it is so easy to turn out of the Church those who by their actions have failed to uphold the standards, and yet to have inside the Church the smug people, the proud people, the prigs and the hypocrites. The Christian Church is never meant to be a society of the moral. No, not a Society of the Moral, but rather a Society of the Forgiven, and of those who put themselves in the way of divine forgiveness, a society ready to carry within its embrace many who have fatally compromised, and all who are unworthy — for all of us are unworthy — the mixed society of those called to be saints.

Let me recall a scene in the Gospel that wonderfully sums up the Church's glory and the Church's scandal. The scene is at the Last Supper. Jesus, there was the glory of the Church, Jesus who is the glory of the Church still, Jesus who judges the Church and heals it and revives it, and sends it on its mission again. Around Jesus there was the scandal of the Church, twelve men, his chosen disciples, engaged in a stupid controversy as to which of them is the greatest. Twelve men professing loyalty and very soon to run away and leave their Master all alone; the scandal of the Church alongside the glory of the Church. And Jesus takes a loaf and blesses it and breaks it and he says 'This is my body.' And he takes the cup of wine and blesses it, and he says 'This is my blood.' And he bids them to eat and he bids them to drink; and they eat and they drink. And he tells them that this is a New Covenant between God and mankind. What did that action really mean? It meant this. Jesus was saying to them 'Tomorrow I am going to die a sacrificial death by crucifixion on Calvary. That death will be an event outside you, indeed outside anybody and everybody, something which men will look at as outside themselves, some from near, some perhaps from far. But now take, eat and drink. The death of Jesus, the total self-offering of Jesus, is to be not only an event outside you, it is to become part of you, it is to be meat and drink within you. Make this my death your food, make it your own, make it the very principle of your life. And here is a sacramental rite given to you in which to the end of time I will be present and I will enable you to make your own, your food and drink, this death that I am going to die.'

The prediction of Jesus was fulfilled, and today whenever the Christian Church meets for the celebration of Eucharist, what happens? Jesus is present in a way that he had wonderfully promised, Jesus risen but once crucified, Jesus so to say still bearing the wounds of his death, still sacrificial, and the Church gathers around Jesus and Jesus feeds the members of the Church with his own death on Calvary. The body broken, the outpoured blood, become the food of the members of the Church so as to be the very stuff and substance of their being in order that through Jesus, and specially through the death of Jesus, they may offer themselves to the glory of God, exhibit the life of Christ to the world, and serve the world in his name. So this Sacrament is everywhere the heart and centre of the life of the Church. It epitomizes the whole range of the Church's life in the worship of God, in the intimacy of its own fellowship and in the pouring out of its own life in the service of humanity.

Now, look at the Church empirically in practice; look round the parish churches in this country, look round the parish churches in other countries, on any continent, and what do we find? In some cases the glory is wonderfully conquering the scandal, it really does happen that the local Christian community is a true authentic fellowship, authentically worshipping God in the depths of its being, and authentically reflecting that worship of God in the very practical caring service of its neighbours. Go to other churches, other parishes: the glory is there because Christ is there, but somehow the scandal has been allowed to swamp the glory and the terrible impotence is apparent. Sometimes the impotence takes the form of just deadness, and sometimes the impotence takes the form of a great concern for worshipping God which is however not reflected in practical service of man, and is therefore a kind of ecclesiaticism and not an authentic worship of the love of God. And sometimes on the other hand the impotence takes the form of a sort of semi-secularized church life in which many efforts are made to pump the Church into efficiency and philanthropy and good works, but the touch with the super-natural is not there. The impotence can both take the form of a false supernaturalism, not expressed in secular concern, but equally the form of a sort of busy secularism in which touch with the supernatural is lost.

I have given a picture of the Church, the glory and the scandal, and it's possible for the glory to conquer the scandal and it's possible elsewhere for the scandal to swamp the glory. And what on our part do we do? Inevitably, because of this situation, we are involved in all the business of criticism and discussion — and there must be criticism if there is to be health, the criticism of Christian people speaking the truth in love, and speaking plainly about this and that and the other which is wrong in the Church of Christ, and trying to put it right; that criticism and that critical spirit simply must be there. But let it always be remembered that the scandal is the scandal of all of us, and the glory is the glory of Christ and Christ alone, and every single Christian is called to reduce his or her own share in keeping the scandal alive by submitting himself or herself more deeply to receive the glory in the Church and to live by it. It is thus that the Church can effectively serve its Lord.

MICHAEL CANTUAR:

Does it matter whether or not Christians are united amongst themselves, or whether such unity as they already have is sufficient?

Those who are called Christians comprise rather less than a third of the world's population, and geographically of course they are unevenly distributed. A hundred years ago we might have considered the question of Christian unity as a domestic problem of the white races. Today it has become a greater problem. Now our horizons are expanded to take in all mankind; now we are living in a world where the limits between races and cultures are disappearing, where at the same time the dominance of the white races and of their cultures is coming to an end. In this wider context we have to ask whether the question of Christian unity has become less urgent because it is less significant than it was, or more urgent. Can I risk suggesting that it has become more urgent? Mankind has reached a stage at which you and I are no longer merely concerned with our own village, our own county, our own country, or our own culture. We are inevitably called upon to be citizens of the world, and the need for human unity is such that without it mankind faces the prospect of mutual destruction. It has been pointed out for instance that the gap and the contrast between the nations who are relatively wealthy and the nations that are relatively poor, unless rational and charitable steps are taken to prevent it, will widen to a point at which there will be no option except to face either internecine war or an imposed domination. We can't afford war today, and we can't bring our consciences in the end to accept the idea of domination. And therefore we have got to seek a solution of our problems from a world point of view. In other words, despite every allowance made for continuing diversity of cultures and with every reservation about political solutions, we can already see that the world (I'm talking now about the world, not just about Christianity) needs to go forward on the path of greater unity.

But if there is one clear lesson of history it is that man does not and cannot live by bread alone. A united humanity that founded its unity only on the basis of economic goods would be what Plato would have called 'a city of pigs', not a human society. All human societies need a purpose and an inspiration, and for Christians there can be no doubt that this human unity to which we are driven to look forward at the present day must be inspired by Christianity, and by the Christian faith, however much our current and temporary Christianity may have to be adapted and adjusted to meet the needs of an age which is strictly without precedent. This is no question for us Christians alone. To the non-Christians we may say: 'What would you substitute for Christianity as the source of inspiration of a unified mankind?' Not science, not philosophy; nor, I think, any other of the religions that exists in the world today, because none of them, as far as we can judge, will be able in the long run, in the longest run, to survive the impact of education and criticism. And Christianity has survived that impact, and is surviving it, not just as the superstition of a retarded group, but as the living faith of men who have assimilated the best that human modern education and criticism can offer.

Unity is a moral force. And therefore the unity of Christendom is a matter not merely of sectional Christian interest but of world-wide importance; and this unity already exists in some measure. It is on the basis of an existing unity that the ecumenical movement found its aspirations and its projects for a more perfect unity. In the narrower horizons of previous centuries each Christian group could assume that the only important issue was to win a victory of controversy over other Christian groups. But today, conscious as we are of a mission field twice as populous as Christendom itself, we Christians are becoming more aware of the things that we share with our fellow Christians, in contrast for the moment with a world which does not yet believe in Christ.

What are our common possessions? Well, in the first place there is something which we share, thank God, with many others who are not Christians, especially with believing Jews and Muslims. That is belief in God. This belief might be held to be the real dividing line between men. And our own Christian Scriptures teach us that 'Whoever fears God and works righteousness is acceptable with God.' A more special link between us Christians is, of course, our faith in Christ the revelation of God, and his disclosure of the ideal of manhood. Then there is the Bible, God's Word expressed in human language. There is baptism, there is the Christian ethic, and the realization of a destiny beyond the grave when we shall know God even as we have been known by him. I think we may add that if, instead of merely listing the features of belief and practice which we Christians hold in common, we try to order our beliefs in a scale of values, we may come to see that what we share in common preponderates infinitely over the things that still seem to divide us from one another.

Now there is a Christian and biblical word for the condition of those who share spiritual blessings in common; and that word is 'communion'. All such sharing is a bond of relationship and a bond of unity. Even outside the religious sphere those who share in a single citizenship are bound to each other by the ties which transcend time and space. And so there is already communion between us Christians, and this real and important unity is something that summons us to a particular kind of mutual charity, that kind of charity that begins at home. We Christians are at home with one another in the possession of spiritual blessings in common. If by baptism we have been incorporated into Christ, then we are indeed brothers with one another. But there is communion, and there is perfect communion, and we have to admit that while we already have a real communion with one another in those supernatural things emanating from Christ which we alike possess, we have not yet got perfect communion. The Fourth Gospel puts on the lips of Christ that prayer for his disciples that 'they may be one as I, Father, and you are one, that the world may know that you have sent me.' The unity of the Church was to show to mankind the divine mission of Christ, and thus the validity of the Christian message and the Christian faith. That sign is blunted, for our communion is imperfect. Perfect communion means that no obstacles exist any longer in faith or practice or discipline, no obstacles to full inter-communion. We know to our cost that such obstacles do exist today, and that the resultant divisions between us are a scandal to the whole world, and hinder men's recognition of the divine origin of Christianity.

I am a Roman Catholic, and Roman Catholics have their own view about this matter of perfect communion. They hold, for instance, that our Lord gave a definite structure to his Church and that that structure, based on Baptism and on the Holy Eucharist, involves an apostolic ministry of bishops grouped round their leader who claims to be the successor of Peter, and that in the communion of that episcopal college a perfect communion is already extant in the world even though it does not yet encompass all baptized persons, still less all who call themselves Christians. No one can deny that the gulf is at present deep between those who accept this Roman Catholic teaching and those who do not. This may help incidentally to explain two facts, both that the Roman Catholic Church for so long a time officially stood aloof from the modern ecumenical movement and also, now that the Roman Catholic Church has moved in on the ecumenical field in a rather big way, that there is a certain amount of hesitation and anxiety amongst the 'old campaigners'. Both these things are true and both are explicable.

But we must not despair of the possibilities of dialogue. Dialogue supposes two things; first that no participant in the dialogue is asked *a priori* to surrender anything that he holds to be of the essence of the 'faith once delivered to the saints', and secondly that all parties to the dialogue in mutual respect agree to take as the starting point of the discussion something that they hold in common. I suggest that while the Roman Catholic idea of perfect communion is not something which all Christians hold in common, the idea of communion, like the fact of communion, is precisely something which is held in common between us, and that here we have the basis for inter-Christian dialogue. This dialogue based on mutual respect needs to be encompassed with prayer because Christian unity is not a mere human achievement, but a gift of God, a gift of grace, and therefore something to be prayed for; and indeed all our efforts towards unity must spring from that cooperation with grace which takes shape as a quest of holiness. It is as you and I, with whatever tears and failures and stumblings, again draw closer through the mercy of God to Christ himself, that we shall inevitably draw closer to each other. Dialogue starts from a respect for diversity of convictions, and a recognition of a common ground from which to start the conversation; but on the other hand we must not be too impatient to dictate to the dialogue its goal, or rather the shape which its goal will take. The Roman Catholic Church's attitude to the ecumenical movement is only one feature of that Church's transformation; but it must obviously be far more difficult to predict the future course of the ecumenical movement itself. Some people are inclined to despair of Christian unity because, they say, 'Well, I don't see how the difficulties could be overcome.' It is not for us to foresee how the difficulties may be overcome. It is a question of the inexhaustible originality of supernatural life and its eternal novelty. The spirit of God bloweth where it listeth and as we know not whence it cometh, so we cannot know whither it goes.

I wish to end with a final note. It can be argued that experience has already shown those who have worked for years in the ecumenical movement that it will not do to seek unity by a mutual shedding of things which we severally but divergently hold to be essential. To shed our differences in that way by dilution of the total content of our faith would be what I call a recourse to the highest common factor (though I am not quite sure whether my mathematics are as good as my theology here). We don't want a reduced Christian gospel. We don't want the kind of 'reunion all round' that the late Ronald Knox satirized — I hasten to add in his pre-Roman Catholic days! It is not as though the best kind of animal were neither a horse nor a kangaroo, nor a lion, but a vague entity without specific differences. What we have to look for is a unity which is I hope of the lowest common multiple type; that is to say, a full gospel richness achieved not by the surrender or the rejection of our several insights, but by sharing of our insights. The values of Protestantism, of Anglicanism, of Eastern Orthodoxy, of Roman Catholicism, are not to be thrown away nor levelled down in an egalitarian fashion but they are to be pooled and made fertile, mutually enriching. So we shall not look back to some impracticable formless Christianity of the past that never was, but we shall look forward to a Christianity so full and rich that it can measure up to the needs of all our denominations, to the needs of the whole of humanity, to the needs of the human spirit which for ever seeks not a point without length or breadth, or depth, but an all-enfolding totality, God himself, One in three persons.

B. C. BUTLER, O.S.B.

A distinction is sometimes made between *the* Gospel and the Social Gospel with the implication that the real business of the Church is the first and not the second, personal conversion and not rehousing; but the distinction is false. There is only one Gospel but as we who claim to accept it live not on desert islands but in societies we must work out its social implications.

The Bible makes clear that God is concerned with the creation as a whole and not merely with individuals, but even if it were exclusively concerned with individual salvation it could not ignore the environment in which the soul matures. The Bible begins in a garden and ends in a city, and both horticulture and civics effect health and growth.

Scripture tells us that Man is made in God's image, by which it presumably means that our faculties of thought, love and reflection are of the same stuff and substance as the faculties of God. And it also means that if we are true to our destiny we shall develop these faculties to reflect God's glory and nature. But man is unlikely to be true to this destiny if he is placed in the wrong soil. Gardeners know that if you want azaleas to grow in a garden you must consider the texture of your soil. And if the azaleas fail to bloom the fault probably lies not with them, but with the garden and the gardener. And we clergy might well ask ourselves when we baptize a child whether the environment in which he is to grow is such that it will be encouraged to honour its baptismal inheritance; for dare the Church which has claimed responsibility for the child's soul disclaim responsibility for his environment?

We hear much of the paganism of the industrial masses, but those of us who have worked in poor parishes are not surprised. Poverty, squalor, illiteracy, hunger, unemployment and racial discrimination do not encourage spiritual development or wholeness of personality. Nor do riches and prosperity. And I know that some clergy think some of the people who sit in their pews are an even greater problem, because although they pay lip service to the Church, their prosperous environment hinders their spiritual vision and dwarfs their personalities. Certainly as we study the history of the last century we are amazed by the ability of some industrialists to be acclaimed as Churchmen although their commercial practices denied their religious professions, jeopardized their souls, brought misery to thousands of their fellow countrymen and shame on the Church. But is it fair to blame them? Like the poor whom they exploited they were victims of their environment, and of an economic system that was rooted in selfishness and greed.

It is important to bear in mind the environmental needs of the rich as well as of the poor, because the Church must be concerned with the whole community and not with a particular section. The gardener takes into consideration the requirements of particular beds, but he is answerable for the whole garden. As Christians we have to work for a state of society in which people can develop their potentialities and achieve their full stature to the glory of God, to the satisfaction of themselves and for the benefit of the community.

Let me give you an illustration from the field of education. A manager of a local school is trying to exercise his or her influence as a Christian; what does this mean? That the children should be given a thorough grounding in Christian Doctrine? Yes. But that is by no means all. If a man is to achieve maturity in the contemporary world he should know something, no matter how simple, of science and of the humanities. Unless both are included in the curriculum the boy or girl will become lop-sided. Hence the point on which I want to insist is that Christian Education is not restricted to the teaching of the Creed and the Catechism; it is concerned with the whole syllabus, because it is the syllabus as a whole, and not just the periods given to religious instruction, that will help to determine a student's development.

And what applies to education applies elsewhere. Housing, recreational facilities, conditions of employment in office and factory, rates of pay, the health service, pensions — all these things determine the environment and affect the growth of personality. And the Church if it is concerned with wholeness, which is what holiness really means, is compelled to be actively interested. To imagine that the Church can proclaim a truncated gospel in a vacuum is to reduce Christianity, which is an all-embracing way of life, to the level of a religious cult. Jesus said that he came to this world to give men abundant life; and it is the obligation of his followers today to carry on his work; to create the conditions that will make it possible for men everywhere to achieve maturity. As Christians we rightly deplore waste. Have you ever considered the appalling waste of talent and skill, of brain and muscle that there is in the world, because the world has not learnt to control its resources and to order its environment?

In the eighth chapter of the Epistle to the Romans, St. Paul tells us that 'the whole creation is on tiptoe to see the wonderful sight of the sons of God coming into their own'. The Church must keep that goal in view and never be content with less.

A second reason for social concern is due to our conviction that people matter as people. If religious conversion is genuine it leads to a double awareness — God and the man next door. We become aware of him because we know that he matters to God. And because he matters to God he must be treated as a personality in his own right, with rights.

I sometimes wish that this apprehension, which contributed so much to the Old Testament prophets, could be as determining in our own thinking. For instance it may so happen that as a result of a housing scheme, a recreational centre, a medical centre, a piece of social service work, that some of those who have been helped will go to church. But scalp-hunting evangelism is not the reason for feeding the hungry, clothing the naked, visiting the sick and the prisoner, and giving water to the thirsty. We do these things because persons are persons, and justice demands it. A churchman must learn to do what is right because it is right without any ulterior motive. If his generous actions awaken a spiritual interest among the people he helps, well and good, but that is something that can be left in God's hands.

A third reason for social concern is pastoral. We clergy instruct young people in the Faith and tell them to obey God and to love their neighbour. Some weeks after their confirmation they may start work. Perhaps they are in an office and are asked to do something which they know is dishonest — to conceal part of the truth, to advertise goods which are not what they claim to be, to put down for expenses items which ought to be entered elsewhere; or they go to a factory and find that pilfering of goods and the fudging of time-sheets may be accepted practices. If they protest they will be told that business is business, and if they do more than protest they may well be asked to go. In some cases the Christian, who perhaps cannot give up his job because of his obligations to his family, accepts the situation and because he is basically honest gives up his churchgoing on the grounds that he won't be a hypocrite; or else he accepts a double standard of morality — one standard for his life as a business executive and another for the Church Council.

I know it is easy to exaggerate the dishonesty in commercial life, but the fact remains that too often the morality of the market place contradicts the morality of the Temple. And because we must be concerned with the growth of the souls committed to the Church's charge, we cannot ignore the world of buying and selling. No system, no regulations, can eradicate dishonesty, but we can strive to create the conditions that will encourage men to be honest.

A fourth reason for social concern is the nature of the Church. And that is the point that I most want to stress. The Church is not an end in itself, but a means to an end. It is God's instrument for the furtherance of this sovereign rule. The Church is not the Kingdom but the agent of it, and a man's primary loyalty is to the Kingdom and not the Church; indeed there have been many times in history when obediance to the *basilica*[1] has necessitated disobedience to the *ecclesia*.

We encounter the word *ecclesia* in classical Greek where it is used to describe the meeting or convocation of the people of the city state to discuss a matter of civic concern with a view to taking action.

In the Bible the *ecclesia* is identified with the people of God who are called by God to take action on his behalf. In the Old Testament the Israelites are the Church.[2]

The emphasis is upon the community, not the individual. It is true that from time to time particular individuals play an important part, but their importance lies in their position in the community. And the community, the Jewish people, are summoned to prepare the way for the Messiah, to lay the foundations of a new ordering of society, to enable the Creator to re-make a shattered creation.

And the Israelites prove their obedience not by putting their signature to doctrinal statements, but by the quality of their commercial life. No matter who wrote the earlier books of the Bible, no matter the precise date, they bear witness to a view of religion which has rarely been equalled. The care of the widow and the orphan, the dispensing of justice, regulations governing land tenure, architecture, and hygiene, a man's obligations towards his neighbours, his duties towards his enemies.

God's purpose was to reconstitute the Creation. He decided to set about reconstituting it within a particular nation. When that had happened the rest of the world could look, and learn and live. But the Jews on the whole preferred another view of religion, not an all-embracing way of life but a culture that rent a man in two and created false distinctions between sacred and secular. Instead of demonstrating belief in the living God by an attitude towards life, they took refuge in ceremonial details and in the worship of high places, with the result that ecclesiasticism came to mean the exact opposite of what was intended; instead of describing a divine concern for life in its totality it described man's absorption in the minutiae of a cultus. And it was against this false view that the prophets waged relentless war. Isaiah, Micah, Hosea, Amos try to call back the Israelites to a proper understanding of God's purposes for them — the *ecclesia*, the people of God, to usher in the Messianic age.

Their success, though limited, was sufficient for Jesus to build upon it. And in the New Testament the good news of God's Kingdom which Jesus taught and portrayed is entrusted to those who are baptized in his name, to the priesthood of all believers. Having reconstituted the creation with himself and having reconciled the warring factions in consequence of his death and resurrection he commissions his Church to continue this work of redemption, the redemption of the entire universal process, with the result that the whole creation is on tiptoe to see the wonderful sight of the sons of God coming into their own.

And the Church is reminded of its calling and of the fact that it is the *ecclesia*, whenever the Holy Communion is celebrated. We, who because of our baptism are the representatives of the New Humanity, take the symbols of creation, bread and wine, and offer them to the Creator together with ourselves, in union with the act of perfect reconciliation effected on Calvary and mediated to us through faithful participation in the Sacrament.

The people of God, gathered at the table of community, are actively engaged in the reconstitution of the creation. As they have taken bread and wine away from the grasping hands of the world and placed them under God's sovereign rule, so they are pledged to bring all life under that rule. The Communion service is a foretaste of the Kingdom. Men are reconciled to one another because they are reconciled to God, and they share together the things of creation because they have first offered them to the Creator. A foretaste but also a pledge, for the Eucharist becomes a meaningless performance, or something worse, unless its rhythm is extended to the whole of life, reconstituting the creation with the Sons of God coming into their own. When the Eucharist becomes an end in itself, when the Church becomes an end in itself, when spiritual experience becomes an end in itself, the Christian faith is debased, God's purposes thwarted, his Kingdom delayed.

To pass from theory to practice. Granted that the function of the Church is, as the Epistle to the Ephesians asserts,[3] to sum up and complete all things in Jesus Christ, what are we to do? How are we to express social concern? How can we help to cultivate the soil for growth?

1.   We must make it known why Christian people should be concerned. It is to me a cause of regret that when clergy express opinions on social matters I (as their Bishop) sometimes get letters of complaint, the writer assuming that a clergyman should not concern himself with such things. In fact the reverse is the case. A Christian – whether he is a clergyman makes no difference – lives in the *polis*.[4] and he must apply his faith to everything that happens in the *polis*. In fact in the strict sense of the word he must be a politician. If for instance, he finds a house on the other side of the road where children are brutally treated, or a school with inadequate facilities, it is his Christian duty to concern himself. He is in the *polis*, they are in the *polis*; they are his neighbours and he must take trouble over their welfare, seeking to bring everything under God's sovereign rule.

2.   In Christian teaching we must distinguish between politics and party politics. If something is to be achieved, political action is required. Talk and well-intentioned resolutions are not enough. For instance if you think that some houses in your neighbourhood are so insanitary as to require demolition you must press for the appropriate political action if anything is to happen. And this is something that churchmen seem loath to admit. One finds general principles, letters to the newspapers, signs of disapproval and concern, but a reluctance to take positive action.

It is true that the Church has a responsibility to stir the national conscience and to influence public opinion by such means as letters to the press and public meetings – in fact we need more, not less – but ultimately what decides the issue is the way a particular committee, council, or Member of Parliament votes.

This does not mean that the Church *qua* Church, should identify itself with political parties. Far from it. But it does mean that individual churchmen, both clerical and lay, should exercise their civic and political rights in accordance with their consciences and insights. To revert to our illustration. We are agreed, let us suppose, that the slums in your neighbourhood should be pulled down and party politics do not enter into the discussion. And suppose the parish priest or minister has done much to bring this about by insisting in addresses, in parish magazines, and in letters to the local press, that people must be decently housed, and has brought matters to a head when after Communion one Sunday morning, he led the entire congregation to wait on the Mayor and local councillors. At first they received the churchpeople rather coldly but when it became clear to them that unless they moved quickly they might lose their seats at the next election they treated them seriously. And now the work is done. But what is to happen to the people who lived in the slums? A Christian has the right and duty to demand that they be given alternative accommodation, but whether the accommodation should be in the same parish or five miles away, and whether the houses should be built by the council or by private enterprise is a party political matter about which we may have our private opinions but which does not concern the Church. And if we think it necessary to express an opinion we must do it as citizens without committing the Church.

3.   It is important that churchmen should be encouraged to serve on local councils and other elected bodies, providing it is made clear from the outset that their political affiliations are their personal concern. I have had a fairly long experience of municipal life, serving on two city councils, and I quickly learnt to respect and admire the devotion and integrity of my fellow councillors irrespective of party. But I sometimes wished that there were more committed Christians among them. In my last parish I stressed this from the pulpit and three members of the congregation responded. Fortunately one was a Conservative, the second a Socialist and the third a Liberal. All stood for election and all won.

It is sometimes argued that the Church should have its own party, as on the Continent. I am sure this would be disastrous. It would be impossible to pass judgement on the credentials of those wanting to join such a party, with the result that the malcontents from other parties and the careerists might force their way in and if mistakes were made, either in personalities or policies, it would bring discontent upon the Church, because the Church as an institution would be held responsible.

Not only is it pride — and a pride that will have a fall — to think that we should have a party of our own and maintain a majestic independence, but it is based on bad theology. A Christian should seek to leaven the lump, and he must not refuse unless he has reason to suppose that the basic aims of the party are incompatible with Christianity.

4. There are dozens of organizations in each area, affecting local people, determining their environment and outlook, in which more church members could be active. It is sad that to many Christians church work means serving on the Parochial Church Council (or similar body), joining the choir, passing around the collecting bag, or arranging the flowers in church. I admit that these jobs must be done. But it is tragic that the laity should think that church work implies the necessity to do something inside a church building. It is possible that they would be of more value to the Church if they were to play an active part in the life of the local community. If there is a church youth club of course it must be staffed; but it may be even more important for members of the congregation to work in the canteen at the town hall on the nights that the hall is used for dancing.

If Christians are to achieve this they must be practical and administratively efficient. In every congregation the church council (or kirk-session, or whatever it is) should have a sub-committee which would be responsible for finding the jobs that needed to be filled and for discovering the people to fill them. It ought to be assumed that each member of the congregation would do something towards maintaining the fabric of local society. Supposing that in church next Sunday everyone were given paper and pencil and invited to write down what they were doing to help the church to make impact upon the life of the area, what sort of response would there be? In fact in the church of which I was Vicar I did issue a questionnaire once a year and those who had nothing to report were asked to volunteer for jobs which were enumerated on the sheet.

5. Christians must remember that no matter how efficient the Welfare State may be there will always be a scope for works of compassion. No government department can legislate adequately for the lonely, the sad, the aged, and the deficient. Works of mercy about which the world knows nothing, are the hallmark of the Christian life. And this is something in which all can engage. Not everyone can serve on city councils, trade unions, or management committees; but all can find opportunities for simple acts of mercy and charity. The man in need is our neighbour and we must love him. Our Lord was involved in great

issues and he confronted the world with his Messianic claims, but a few hours before he was put to death on a political charge he let the disciples into the secret of his ministry by washing their feet. Feet-washing takes time and lacks glamour, bur feet-washers we must be.

Recently a woman I had confirmed told me that what had brought her into the Church was the welcome that she and her family had received on the day they had entered their new council house. Somebody from the congregation provided a meal and brought flowers. The sense of loneliness went; they knew they were among friends.

6.   My last point concerns immediate issues and the need for the Church to face them, to give a lead and not to run away from them.

Most people are not moved by the proclamation of general moral principles in a vacuum, but they become interested when the principles are applied to particular situations. And quite right too. For what is the point of preaching the Gospel unless it compels listeners to make up their minds and take sides. In fact, if people do not take sides, but are allowed to slumber in a smug lethargy, it is safe to assume that the Gospel of Jesus is not being preached. Christians must decide what are the vital issues in any particular situation, and then take action. To run away from these vital issues is to be guilty of cowardice and to bring the Church into contempt. And to confine ourselves to pious generalizations is to lay ourselves open to the charge of hypocrisy.

In season and out of season we are told that the Church should give a lead, but how can the Church lead unless, like the prophets of old, it relates eternal truths to contemporary situations? Our task is not to supply the spiritual varnish for the status quo, but to expose what is incompatible with the will of God and to encourage the compatible. That is the only way to hasten the acceptance of God's sovereignty.

MERVYN SOUTHWARK

[1] The *basilica* (from Greek *basilikos*, royal) was a type of building used in the Roman Empire for the sessions of courts of justice and other state business. The *basilica* is therefore the place where the justice of the Kingdom (*basileia*) is dispensed and this can stand for the heavenly as well as the earthly kingdom.

[2] 'For thou art a holy people unto the Lord thy God, and the Lord hath chosen thee to be a peculiar people unto himself, above all the nations of the earth' (Deut. 14:2).

'When Israel was a child, then I loved him, and called my son out of Egypt' (Hos. 11:1). Compare Acts 7:38, 'the church (*ecclesia*) in the wilderness'.

[3] Eph. 1:9—10.

[4] The *polis* (Greek for 'city') is the 'political' community. The ancient Greek city-state was small enough for every citizen (*politēs*) to take part in the assembly (in Greek, *ecclesia*) which decided by vote on matters of state, as Parliament does with us.

Appendix
Contents of Part I

Index of Contributors to Parts I and II
with biographical notes

William Barclay, C.B.E., D.D., Professor of Divinity and Biblical Criticism, Glasgow University, since 1963 . . *Part I, p.* 128
Formerly Lecturer in New Testament Language and Literature, Glasgow University.

A. C. F. Beales, D.Lit., Professor of the History of Education, King's College, University of London since 1965. Fellow of King's College, London. . . . . *Part II, p.* 27
Formerly Lecturer in History and in Education, University College, Swansea, and Talks Producer, B.B.C. Became an R.C. in 1935.

The Rt. Rev. Christopher Butler, O.S.B., LL.D., Auxiliary Bishop to the Cardinal Archbishop of Westminster since 1966. President, St. Edmund's College, Ware, since 1968, and Hon. Fellow of St. John's College, Oxford. . . . . *Part II, p.* 113
Formerly Headmaster of Downside School and Abbot of Downside.

David Cairns, D.D., Emeritus Professor of Practical Theology, Aberdeen University. . . . . *Part II, p.* 1
Formerly Chaplain, Scots Guards.

The Most Rev. Donald Coggan, D.Litt., D.D., S.T.D., Archbishop of York since 1961; Pro-Chancellor York and Hull Universities.
Part I, p. 1
Formerly Bishop of Bradford.

Thomas Corbishley, S.J., formerly Master of Campion Hall, Oxford and Superior of Farm Street Church, London. . . *Part I, p.* 36

C. A. Coulson, Ph.D., D.Sc., F.R.S., Rouse Ball Professor of Mathematics, Oxford University, and Fellow of Wadham College, Oxford, since 1952. . . . . *Part I, p.* 79
Formerly Fellow of Trinity College, Cambridge and Professor of Theoretical Physics, King's College, London.

A. C. Craig, M.C., D.D., formerly Chaplain of Glasgow University and Lecturer in Biblical Studies, Glasgow University, and Moderator of the General Assembly of the Church of Scotland, 1961-62.
Part II, p. 98

Charles L. Warr, G.C.V.O., D.D., LL.D., F.R.S.E., late Dean of the Chapel Royal in Scotland and of the Order of the Thistle, and Minister of St. Giles' Cathedral. . . . . . . *Part I, p.* 101

H. A. Williams, M.A., Community of the Resurrection since 1969.
                                                   Part II, p. 71
Formerly Fellow and Chaplain of Trinity College, Cambridge; Chaplain and Tutor of Westcott House, Cambridge.

The Rt. Rev. Ronald Selby Wright, C.V.O., T.D., D.D., Minister of the Canongate (The Kirk of Holyroodhouse) and Edinburgh Castle. Chaplain to H.M. the Queen in Scotland. Moderator of the General Assembly of the Church of Scotland, 1972-73.   *Editor*

Edward Yarnold, S.J., Master of Campion Hall, Oxford.   *Part II, p.* 9

Subject index